Success with Sensory Supports

of related interest

Sensory Stories to Support Additional Needs
Making Narratives Accessible Through the Senses
Joanna Grace
Forewords by Martyn Sibley and Flo Longhorn
ISBN 978 1 83997 147 1
eISBN 978 1 83997 148 8

Sensory Solutions in the Classroom
The Teacher's Guide to Fidgeting, Inattention and Restlessness
Monique Thoonsen and Carmen Lamp
Illustrated by Ruud Bijman
Foreword by Winnie Dunn
ISBN 978 1 78592 697 6
eISBN 978 1 78592 698 3

Sensory and Motor Strategies (3rd edition)
Practical Ways to Help Autistic Children and Young People Learn and Achieve
Corinna Laurie
Illustrated by Kirsteen Wright
ISBN 978 1 83997 272 0
eISBN 978 1 83997 271 3

The Kids' Guide to Staying Awesome and In Control
Simple Stuff to Help Children Regulate their Emotions and Senses
Lauren Brukner
ISBN 978 1 84905 997 8
eISBN 978 0 85700 962 3

Simple Stuff to Get Kids Self-Regulating in School
Awesome and In Control Lesson Plans, Worksheets, and Strategies for Learning
Lauren Brukner and Lauren Liebstein Singer
Illustrated by John Smission
ISBN 978 1 78592 761 4
eISBN 978 1 78450 623 0

Success with Sensory Supports

The Ultimate Guide to Using Sensory Diets, Movement Breaks and Sensory Circuits at School

Kim Griffin

Jessica Kingsley Publishers
London and Philadelphia

First published in Great Britain in 2023 by Jessica Kingsley Publishers
An imprint of John Murray Press

1

Copyright © Kim Griffin 2023
Foreword copyright © Dr Emma Goodall 2023

All internal images © GriffinOT
Sense illustrations by Frances Coles
Other illustrations by Rebecca Ball

All sections marked with ★ can be downloaded at https://library.jkp.com/redeem
using the voucher code VYASPAL for personal use with this programme, but may
not be reproduced for any other purposes without the permission of the publisher.

A CIP catalogue record for this title is available from the
British Library and the Library of Congress

ISBN 978 1 83997 191 4
eISBN 978 1 83997 192 1

Printed and bound in Great Britain by CPI Group Ltd

Jessica Kingsley Publishers' policy is to use papers that are natural,
renewable and recyclable products and made from wood grown in
sustainable forests. The logging and manufacturing processes are expected
to conform to the environmental regulations of the country of origin.

Jessica Kingsley Publishers
Carmelite House
50 Victoria Embankment
London EC4Y 0DZ

www.jkp.com

John Murray Press
Part of Hodder & Stoughton Limited
An Hachette UK Company

Contents

Introduction

Hello readers! My name is Kim Griffin. I'm an occupational therapist who has been supporting sensory needs for the last 20 years. Over this time, I have seen the availability and use of sensory supports increase tenfold.

Nowadays, most educators will have heard of the term sensory diet, and they may have access to a few pieces of sensory equipment at school. **I am excited that sensory needs are being recognized and more frequently supported in classrooms.** However, I am acutely aware that there is a gap between availability of sensory supports and training in how to use them. For example, 91 per cent of participants on my own course report that they use sensory supports, but only 24 per cent report that they have had training.[1]

This concerns me, as sensory supports are not toys. **To be effective, sensory supports must be selected and used correctly.** It is important to ensure that those using sensory strategies understand the benefits and risks. My goal with this book is to give you a step-by-step reasoning process which will allow you to use these strategies safely and effectively. Thank you for making the time to increase your sensory awareness with me.

A sensory addition

This book is designed to help you **understand the world of sensory supports**. It is written to help you understand sensory needs and behaviours. It will enable you to identify sensory needs and use sensory tools more effectively. It will add sensory awareness to your toolbox.

However, the book is **not designed as a diagnostic tool**. The information

---

1   Griffin & Allen (2021) Auditing the impact of online sensory processing training for educators, families, and professionals. Available at: https://www.griffinot.com/the-impact-of-sensory-processing-with-griffin-ot

should be used alongside professional advice you have been given for individual children. If you are ever unsure or need additional help for individual children, please seek additional advice from your local health professionals. Occupational therapists can help with specific sensory needs, but, depending on their needs, the child may also need help from a speech therapist, psychologist or paediatrician.

Book structure

The book is divided into six chapters. **It is designed to be read in order.** I know that you will be tempted to just jump to Chapter 5, as it contains the strategies. I know you are keen to get started helping. However, I promise that reading Chapters 1–4 first will be time very well spent. These chapters will give you the understanding you need to use the strategies in Chapter 5 to effectively meet the needs of the children you are supporting.

Chapter outline

- Chapter 1 introduces the eight senses. Knowledge of the eight senses will help you understand which sense specific strategies are targeting.

- Chapter 2 explores regulation. Regulation is a key goal of using sensory supports. It is essential that you understand regulation so that you can choose supports correctly.

- Chapter 3 explains how to evaluate sensory needs and set goals. It outlines how you can identify sensory triggers for behaviours and how to understand an individual child's sensory profile.

- Chapter 4 describes how you can use the information gathered in your evaluation to make a sensory plan.

- Chapter 5 contains the sensory strategies. I explore equipment, specific activities and how these can be combined into sensory circuits and sensory diets.

- Chapter 6 considers how you can teach children to use their sensory strategies independently to support self-regulation.

Case studies

As you read through the book you will meet **Isla** and **Noah**. Their stories will be used to help illustrate how the information in this book can be used practically. Excerpts from their stories are used in the book, but you can read their full stories in the Appendix at the end of the book.

Icons

Throughout the book, you will see the following icons. These will give you more information or tips on the topics being discussed.

 Note from Kim – a personal anecdote, or reinforcement of a key piece of information on the page from Kim.

 Practical example – an example of how to use the information in real life.

 Learn more – links to books or other resources for further reading to learn more about the topic.

 Reflective practice – questions readers can use to consider how they can apply the information.

 Teacher perspective – contribution by Dr Emma Goodall explaining how a teacher might use or has used or applied the information in the classroom.

 Safety flag – precautions and things to consider to ensure the child and adult are safe.

Appendix

The Appendix at the end of the book contains tools and checklists that you can download online at https://library.jkp.com/redeem using the voucher code VYASPAL. These sections are clearly marked with ★ and are for personal use with this programme, but may not be reproduced for any other purposes without the permission of the publisher.

There are also additional resources available on www.GriffinOT.com/success which include video training and also downloads of the images in various formats.

Foreword

DR EMMA GOODALL

This interesting book provides a foundational knowledge of the senses and how sensory differences can impact children and young people. Educators and families will find it helpful to read through the whole book to gain an understanding of why some children and young people behave in the ways that they do. This book is fundamental to being able to plan and use sensory strategies effectively in the home, community and school.

The author presents all eight senses and explains the different kinds of sensory atypicality as well as introducing how autism, attention deficit hyperactivity disorder (ADHD) and dyspraxia impact both sensory processing and arousal levels. Words that may be perceived as occupational therapy jargon are explained well so that interpreting sensory reports will be much easier after reading this book.

Chapter 1

Introducing the Senses

'Sensations create the foundation of our experiences.'

Like all animals, humans use sensations to understand the world. Sensations give the brain critical information about our environment and our own body. Our brains rely on sensory feedback to make decisions throughout the day.

The chapter will explore the senses in further depth. I will introduce the eight senses and the concept of sensory processing. I will also consider how the brain processes the sensory messages and why using sensory supports can be helpful for some children.

My sensory world

One of **my favourite** sensory experiences is standing on a white sandy beach on a warm summer's day. I love the sound of waves crashing on the shore. I love the feeling of sand in between my toes and the squeaking sound it makes when I walk across it. I love to watch the waves swell and crash, and the smell of the salt in the air. I love to feel the waves crash into my skin when I go swimming in the water. I even like the taste of the salt. This type of beach is one of my favourite sensory experiences.

This **contrasts significantly** with standing on a pebbled beach. I hate the sound of the waves crashing on the pebbles and the grinding sound they make when they are rolling back away from the shore. I hate the feeling of walking on pebbles – they hurt my feet. I don't even take my shoes off. I never make it into the water, as the idea of walking over the pebbles puts me off. The one similarity is the smell and taste of the salt, but this is not enough to make it enjoyable for me!

While I've focused on **external** sensory messages when painting these pictures, my brain also receives information from my **internal** senses each time I go to the beach. The sensory messages from my vestibular and proprioceptive senses enable me to walk and swim. My internal senses tell me when I'm hungry and should stop for some food, and they let me know if I need to find a toilet or some shade.

A trip to the beach

Our sensory world

The world is one big sensation. Our bodies are constantly receiving external and internal sensory messages. Our brains continually process these messages. These sensations help us to make sense of our own body and the world.

Even **when we are asleep**, our brain knows we are lying down. It wakes us up if we get a message from our bladder saying it's full. It wakes us up if we hear an unfamiliar (or familiar in the case of a baby crying) sound. It also makes sure we don't fall out of bed when we roll over!

There is **no escaping** these sensory messages. They come from both the external world and inside our own bodies. They are everywhere. Some children[1] (and adults) find processing these messages more challenging than others.

Note from Kim

While the senses will now be presented separately to aid your understanding, the reality is that **they rarely work in isolation**. The brain is constantly receiving and processing multiple sensory messages at the same time from different senses. This helps our brain to build a complete picture of both our external and internal worlds.

External world sensations

Our external world senses receive sensations from outside our body. They receive sensory messages from the environment and those that are in it. These are the five senses that you will have been taught at school and will be familiar with.

Taste (gustatory)

The sense of **taste** receives sensory messages from our tongue. Different parts of our tongue respond to different flavours, like sweet, salty, sour, bitter and umami. A chemical reaction occurs when flavours touch the tongue. This lets the brain know the taste of the food, or other item, that is in our mouth. It helps us to know if food is safe to eat.

---

1   I will use the term children/child throughout this book. However, most of the concepts are applicable to teenagers and adults as well!

Smell (olfactory)

The sense of **smell** receives sensory messages through our nose. Like taste, the sense of smell is a chemical reaction. Different scents enter the nose, and our body converts these to chemical signals that the brain can process. This lets us smell the differences between scents, for example the smell of a flower compared to sewerage.

Vision

Our sense of **vision** receives sensory messages from the eyes. Unlike other animals, humans can only process visual images when there is light available. In darkness, we cannot see. There are different receptors at the back of our eyes that process shapes, colour and movement. These sensory messages are sent to the brain for further interpretation.

Our sense of vision lets us see the world. It alerts us to potential dangers up ahead. It helps us to identify objects and read signs. Vision also helps us navigate around our environment without bumping into things and getting lost. It helps us to read the non-verbal cues when we are with others. The sense of vision also supports balance and hand-eye coordination.

Hearing (auditory)

The ears are responsible for processing the **sounds** we hear in our environment. Inside the ear is a section called the cochlea. It is responsible for processing sound waves. Sound waves enter the ear and make the ear drum vibrate. The brain interprets these vibrations as sounds.

Our sense of hearing tells us which direction sounds are coming from. It alerts us to danger and supports verbal communication. It also lets us listen to our favourite piece of music or podcast.

Touch (tactile)

The **touch** sense processes sensory **messages from the skin**. The skin is the largest organ of the human body. Anything that touches the skin will activate the touch receptors. There are receptors for:

- touch

- pressure

- vibration

- pain

- temperature.

Different parts of the body are more sensitive than others. This is because **each body part has a different number of touch receptors**. Receptors are the cells in the body that receive the sensory information. The hands, face and mouth have more receptors than the feet and back. This gives them greater sensitivity and coordination (or dexterity).

Our sense of touch gives us rich information about the **details of objects**. What shape are they? Are they hot or cold? Are they soft, hard or textured? Touch also helps to protect us from danger; for example, if we touch a hot surface our hand will pull away.

Two-touch sensations

It is very helpful to understand that the skin processes two different types of touch sensory information. One plays a protective role, the other facilitates our dexterity. There are different receptors which take information to different parts of the brain:

- *Protective touch:* This is a light touch sensation; for example, a spider web touching your skin, or hair touching your face. As the name suggests, protective touch plays a **key role in keeping us safe, or protecting us**. This type of touch is very alerting and can produce a fight, flight or freeze response.

- *Discriminative touch:* This part of our touch system provides **very specific and detailed information** about what we are touching or where we have been touched. It helps us to understand the shape and texture of items. It facilitates our fine motor skills and dexterity. The discriminative touch system allows me to type the words of this book into my keyboard (along with my proprioceptors, which you will learn about in a moment).

Thinking back to my sandy beach, it is my **discriminative** touch receptors that feel the sand between my toes. I like this feeling. If I happen to step on a sharp piece of shell, my **protective** touch receptors will react and tell my body to lift my foot up immediately. The receptors work side by side to help keep me safe and let me enjoy the sensations of the sand.

Internal body sensations

Our internal senses receive their sensory **messages from inside the body**, rather than immediately from the external world. The proprioceptive and vestibular senses are activated by movement. The interoceptive sense is always working in the background.

Proprioception (body position)

Proprioception is often called our 'hidden sixth sense'. It lets the brain know where our limbs are in space and how they are moving. Essentially, **proprioception helps you to 'feel' where your body is**. For example, when you walk, you do not have to look at your feet to know where they are.

Your proprioceptive sense 'feels' your legs and feet and lets your brain know where they are.

The receptors for the proprioceptive sense are in our **muscles and joints**. This is different from the touch sense, which receives sensory inputs from the skin. The proprioceptive sense receives information about:

- **muscle stretch**, which tells the brain if the joints are open or closed and what position the joints are in

- **joint loading and joint compression**, which tells the brain how much pressure is on the joints. For example, if you are carrying something heavy, more pressure will be on your joints, compared to if you are holding something light, or nothing at all.

The proprioceptive sense helps us with every movement our body makes. It makes sure our body is in the **right position**. It helps us to **push and pull** with the **right amount of force** or pressure. Proprioceptive feedback allows us to be successful with both simple and complex movements.

When I type, my **touch** sense feels the keys when I touch them. However, before I can touch them, my **proprioceptors** move my fingers to the correct key. Touch typing is really a misnomer – *proprioceptive typing* is technically the more accurate description!

My proprioceptors are also responsible for pressing the keys hard enough to make them respond, but not so hard that I damage my keyboard. I am typing on a relatively new laptop, so I don't need to use a lot of force. However, if I was typing on my old keyboard, I would have needed to use more pressure. My proprioceptors make these adjustments automatically.

Practical example

Have you ever had a child in your class who just can't seem to **keep their body in their own space**? When they reach for the glue stick, they bump into the child sitting next to them. When they use the glue stick, they use much pressure. Their materials often end up on the floor as they accidentally knock them off. Carpet time is also tricky as they keep touching the other children around them. It is highly likely that this child is not effectively processing the sensory inputs from their proprioceptors.

Vestibular (balance)

The vestibular sense is usually called the **balance sense**. The receptors for the vestibular sense are in the middle ear, after the cochlea, in a section called the vestibule. The receptors are activated by **head movement**. They tell the brain **how fast** the head is moving, in **which direction** and **how high** it is off the ground. The one external sensory message the vestibular sense receives is the pull of **gravity**.

Adequate processing of vestibular sensory messages is essential for:

- balance
- coordination
- attention
- stillness
- eye movements
- alertness and attention.

The vestibular sense is also the one that makes you feel sick if you have had too much movement. Everyone has different thresholds of how much movement they can tolerate. Some people love the idea of fast rollercoasters, others hate them. This is because their vestibular sense processes the information differently.

Interoception

This is the final internal sense. The interoceptive sense **processes internal sensory messages** received from our organs, hormones and immune system. These messages tell the brain **what's going on inside the body** and help it to understand the **body's internal state**.

Interoceptive sensory messages could be about:

- hunger (or fullness)

- need for the toilet

- tiredness

- internal stress or heightened arousal

- pain/discomfort

- internal temperature

- feelings and emotions.

When we have good interoceptive awareness, we notice the impact that external sensory messages have on our internal state. For example, I know if I get lost when driving, my arousal increases. If the radio is on (auditory input), I become even more stressed. If I turn the radio off, this helps to lower my arousal and anxiety. The external sounds from the radio negatively affect my internal state. And when my internal arousal state is higher, I am less tolerant of external sensory messages.

Interoception vs external sensory messages

Let's use the auditory sense as an example. Our sense of **hearing** hears external sounds in the environment. But if we have a cold or earache, it is our **interoceptive sense** that notices that internal pain and discomfort. It's the same with stomach pain or headache, the interoceptors tell the brain that there is discomfort in the body.

Temperature is another good example. If the **air temperature** is hot, the touch sense will feel the external temperate on the skin. But if we become too hot from sitting in the sun, it is our interoceptors that notice **the internal body temperature rise**. If we take notice of this discomfort and move out of the sun, we may avoid getting sunstroke. However, if we don't notice the signals from our body, there is a high chance we will have a headache later in the day.

Reflective practice

It's your turn. Think of one of your favourite places to be and reflect on the sensory messages your brain is receiving. Try to come up with at least one thing for each of the eight senses. You can grab a notebook, use your computer or jot your ideas down right here!

My favourite place: . . . .

The sensations I am receiving:

Taste: . . . .

Smell: . . . .

Vision: . . . .

Sounds: . . . .

Touch: . . . .

Proprioceptive: . . . .

Vestibular: . . . .

Interoception: . . . .

Sensory processing explored

Sensory processing is an **umbrella term** which explores how the brain interprets the sensory messages it receives. It includes:

- the brain's ability to notice the sensation (sensory registration)
- the brain's ability to interpret the sensation (sensory discrimination)
- how intensely the brain notices and responds to the information (responsivity/modulation)
- how the brain uses sensory feedback to coordinate movement (praxis and posture).

When I use the term sensory processing in this book, I am referring to how the brain interprets all the sensory messages it receives. Some children have **an impairment with their sensory organs**, for example they might have reduced sight or hearing. These children are not receiving adequate or complete sensory messages in the first place. They will require specialist supports such as glasses or hearing aids.

The children this book is written for *do not* have impairments with their sensory organs. Their eyes and ears are receiving the sensory messages just fine. However, **their brain does not interpret the sensory messages in the same way as their peers' brains**. Their brain may not notice sensations, it might feel sensations more intensely, or it may not be able to organize the sensory messages to produce coordinated movement.

Sensory integration and sensory strategies: a note on terminology

I am using the term sensory processing within this book as it is a more widely recognized term. However, the term would not exist in its current form without the work of a therapist named A. Jean Ayres. Ayres' theory of **sensory integration** (Ayres 1973) laid the foundation for all future generations of occupational therapists studying the senses. She created a treatment approach – Ayres® Sensory Integration Therapy – which is still used by trained therapists today.

Her work also inspired the **sensory strategies** that you will learn in this book. Sensory strategies include any supports or equipment that use the senses to help a child (or adult) participate successfully. You will learn a lot more about sensory strategies in Chapters 3–5 of this book. I just want to differentiate them from Ayres® Sensory Integration Therapy here to help with your understanding.

A note on diagnosis

At the time of writing, sensory processing disorder and sensory integrative dysfunction are **not formally recognized medical diagnoses**. The terms are widely used and sometimes written in professional reports, but they are not recognized within the official diagnostic manuals, the *Diagnostic and Statistical Manual of Mental Disorders, fifth edition* (DSM-5) and the *International Classification of Diseases, 11th edition* (ICD-11). This is why sensory processing is sometimes not recognized by health authorities, particularly in the UK, and may not be covered under insurance, for example in the USA.

Sensory hyper- and hypo-responsivity are included within the autistic spectrum disorder diagnosis. The current guidelines from the National Institute for Health and Care Excellence (NICE) (2017) recommend that an assessment of sensory differences should take place for autistic individuals. However, in my experience, this recommendation has not yet been widely adopted in the UK.

The recognized diagnostic term for dyspraxia is **developmental coordination disorder** (DCD). DCD is included in the DSM-5 and the ICD-11 as a recognized diagnosis. It frequently occurs alongside other neurodiversities such as dyslexia, ADHD and autism (Kirby & Sugden 2007). Historically, having an autism diagnosis precluded a diagnosis of DCD (DSM-IV), but this is no longer the case.

Note from Kim

Terminology can be very confusing. You will frequently read the diagnosis of 'sensory processing disorder' in professional reports, even though it is not a formal diagnosis. Some therapists will use the term sensory integration dysfunction. While there is some research indicating sensory processing may be a standalone diagnosis, at the time of writing there is insufficient evidence for it to be included in diagnostic manuals.

Sensory registration

This refers to the moment the **brain registers or recognizes** that a sensation has occurred. Registration is the 'ah ha!' moment – the moment the brain notices the sensation. The brain must **register** the sensory message **first**, before it can process it. Some children take longer to register or notice a sensation than others.

Sensory discrimination

This means processing of the **qualities of the sensory message**. It refers to what, how and where. What was the sensation? How intense was it? Where did it occur?

Let's look at an example using the sense of **hearing**. Your brain **registers a sound**. Then, it starts to process the **qualities of the sound**. Is it familiar or not? What does it sound like (a bird, a dog, a bell, a siren)? Was it loud or soft? It also processes the **direction of the sound**. Was it nearby or far away? Was it on your right, your left, in front or behind you? As the brain answers these questions, it **discriminates the qualities** of the sound.

The brain is constantly discriminating the qualities of sensory messages. This is how we understand and **attach meaning to the sensory world**. We use sensory discrimination all the time to **adjust our**

own movements. For example, when we squeeze toothpaste from the tube, we adjust the amount of pressure depending on how empty or full the tube is. As we squeeze, we adjust the position we hold the tube, and we stop squeezing when we see there is enough toothpaste on the brush. Sensory discrimination helps us to perform the task successfully. If we don't use the right amount of force, or judge that there is already enough toothpaste, we will have too little or too much toothpaste.

Sensory reactivity

Sensory reactivity[2] refers to the **intensity** with which an individual's **brain interprets** the sensory messages it receives. Everyone has different thresholds for sensory information, and this influences how their brain reacts. **Reactivity affects our responses** and our capacity to respond to and engage with learning. Some authors call sensory reactivity **sensory modulation**.

If you have ever been in a room where you have heard a sound, for example a phone or doorbell ringing, that someone else didn't, you have seen **different reactivity thresholds** in action. Maybe you were the person who didn't hear the phone. The **volume of the sound was identical** for both people, but their **brains' reactivity thresholds were different**. The person who heard the sound had a lower reactivity threshold and their brain heard the sound more readily.

Another sound example is when a baby cries at night. The **volume** of the baby's cry is **identical** for all carers in the house. However, many, not all, mothers will say that their partner doesn't stir when the baby cries. This is another example of sensory reactivity thresholds. The person who hears the cries and wakes first has a lower reactivity threshold to the sound and notices it first. The person who does not stir has a higher reactivity threshold to the sound.

While there is a 'typical range', studies indicate that 5–15 per cent of the population react to sensory messages in a different way to their peers. Reactivity to sensory messages can be either more sensitive (hyper) or less sensitive (hypo). Some children also have difficulty ignoring irrelevant sensory messages, so they continually notice micro sensations that others ignore.

---

2   Different authors will use different terms, like modulation (Lucy Miller) and responsivity (Winnie Dunn).

SENSITIVITY (OVER-RESPONSIVITY/HYPER-REACTIVITY)

When there is **sensitivity**, the brain interprets sensory messages with **a greater level of intensity**. The terms over-responsivity and hyper-reactivity are also used to describe sensitivity to sensory inputs. Some authors (e.g., Winnie Dunn) also include a category of 'avoiding'.

Let's use **sound** again as an example. If a child is sensitive to sounds, their brains will likely hear sounds in the distance that yours don't. Their brains are likely to be quickly overwhelmed by the sound of the school bell, because to them it is not a low volume sound, it is deafening and painful. The lunchtime playground whistle will likely sound the same.

The child's response might be to **avoid** those situations. They might **act out** by running away or becoming aggressive; or they could **internalize their distress** and shut down (this is called sensory overload). Each of these is a **valid response** to a sensation that causes distress. However, this can stop a child from participating, put the child in an unsafe situation, or, in the case of aggression, get them into trouble. Sensory strategies, particularly environmental modifications, can help to support these children.

SLOWER (UNDER-RESPONSIVITY/HYPO-REACTIVITY)

Slowness to sensory responses (under-responsivity/hypo-reactivity) is the opposite. The brain is **slower to interpret sensory messages** as it perceives them with less intensity. These children often need **more sensory inputs** to process the information. Sometimes they will **seek out** additional sensory inputs themselves.

Let's consider an example with the **vestibular** (balance) sense. When children are slower to respond to vestibular sensory messages, they can be sluggish and slow to become alert. Because their brain processes the change in head movement that lets them know that they are losing their balance more slowly, they may fall over more easily. They may even fall off their chair or bed because they don't notice they have moved over the edge.

Some children might **move about a lot**, because they are pro-actively trying to get the extra movement that will help to increase their alertness. They are often called sensory seekers. It can be helpful to separate out the two responses to slower processing, as sensory supports for the children need to be implemented differently.

Slower responses are grouped differently by different authors. Winnie Dunn (1999), the first author to create a specific assessment tool for sensory modulation, grouped slower responses into seeking and under-responsive. She felt this reflected the different responses a child might have if their brain was slower to process the sensory input. Lucy Miller (2014) has more recently used the term craving instead of seeking. The autism diagnostic criteria and the updated Ayres® Sensory Integration model only include hypo-reactivity (Bundy & Lane 2019).

Sensory movement (dyspraxia and posture)

The final piece of the sensory processing puzzle is **movement**. This includes **dyspraxia** and **posture**. Dyspraxia is difficulty planning, organizing and sequencing new movements or activities. Posture relates to postural control, balance and stability. It is common for children with discrimination and/or reactivity difficulties to also have movement difficulties. Coordinated movement requires excellent processing of the sensory messages our brain receives. When these messages aren't being adequately processed, it is harder for the brain to produce coordinated movement.

Sensory strategies support reactivity

Sensory strategies primarily support **sensory reactivity**. They can be used to help children avoid sensory overload. They can enable a child to have greater **control over their own responses**. They can be used to help prepare children for activities they might otherwise find overwhelming, and to aid a child in **maintaining focused attention**. This book aims to teach you the fundamentals of using sensory strategies with children who need extra support to regulate.

Learn more

Kim's free introductory training explores the senses and sensory processing in further depth. You can join it here: www.griffinot.com/sensory-processing-disorder-training.

These books explore sensory processing in further depth:

♦ *Sensory Processing Challenges: Effective Clinical Work with Kids and Teens* by Lindsey Biel (2014, W.W. Norton & Company)

- *Living Sensationally: Understanding Your Senses* by Winnie Dunn (2007, Jessica Kingsley Publishers)

- *Sensational Kids: Hope and Help for Children with Sensory Processing Disorder (SPD).* Revised by Lucy Miller (2014, TarcherPerigee)

This book is particularly good for parents:

- *The Out-of-Sync Child* by Carol Kranowitz (2005, Penguin Putnam)

Reflective practice

Let's think about your own reactions to sensations.

- Can you think of an example when you may have reacted to sensations in the environment differently to others?

- Are there any specific sensations that you deliberately avoid?

- Are there any specific sensations that you deliberately seek out?

- Are there sensations that you find calming?

- What sensations, if any, do you find extremely irritating?

Teacher perspective – Dr Emma Goodall

Sensory differences and difficulties are at the heart of many struggles experienced by children and young people in school. It is really important for educators to be aware of **the range of sensory issues experienced by their students** in order to implement a range of strategies that will minimize the stress or distress that some sensory experiences can cause these students.

Common sensory challenges, like an aversion to the school bell, are fairly easily recognized. However, a student who is unable to focus when sitting directly under the light may have their **sensory sensitivity unrecognized or misinterpreted**. Instead of removing the light bulb or moving the student, it is possible the teacher will assume the young person is simply work avoiding or has some other reason for not focusing.

It can be difficult for teachers to provide the perfect mix of sensory strategies when their class may contain a **mix of students who have polar opposite support needs**. One student may be unable to bear the sound of a pencil moving across paper, while another cannot focus unless there is significant noise or movement. Yet another student needs personal space, while another requires deep pressure to feel calm.

The complex mix of hypo- and hyper-sensory registration and reactivity is **further complicated by their changeability**. A student who is noise sensitive to the school bell and classroom chatter may make constant noise themselves by tapping on the table, perhaps to try and blur out the other noises or because they are sensory seeking a particular sensation that they can get by tapping the table.

A common challenge faced by teachers is when a student says it is too noisy, even though to the teacher the classroom sounds quiet. This type of student may be hearing noises that the teacher cannot hear, or the noise from the class next door, or the traffic outside. **The differences in sensory experiences between those with and without sensory processing difficulties are quite amazing.**

As a neurodivergent teacher, I have long understood these students with sensory processing difficulties because I share them. Just like these students, I can focus and work most effectively when my environment is tailored to my needs, or at least accommodates my key sensory reactivities.

Chapter 2

Understanding Regulation

'To use sensory strategies successfully, you must first understand arousal and regulation.'

This chapter of the book explores **arousal** and **regulation**. Understanding these concepts will help you to know why you are using sensory supports. They will help you to identify when a child might need help, and which type of sensory support will be the best one to use with them.

There is no **one size fits all** for sensory supports. Sensory integration therapists complete post-graduate training to fully understand the nuances. The brain is complicated. There are many areas to consider. This chapter explores the fundamentals so you will have a basic understanding.

Note from Kim

I know your priority is to know WHAT to do, what the strategies are. However, I have put this chapter first very deliberately. It is my firm belief that you need to understand the WHY first. When you understand the WHY, you know how to choose the correct WHAT. And you will be aware of how to use that WHAT safely and correctly.

Arousal

Arousal refers to the **level of energy and alertness** in the body. At its simplest, it is how **alert or asleep your body is** in any given moment. Arousal levels impact attention, engagement and learning. We can use strategies, including sensory supports, to change our level of arousal.

It's common to see thermometers, ladders or steps used to represent arousal. Low arousal is typically at the bottom and high arousal is at the top. Between this, there are increments to indicate the changes from low to high. Usually there is a space in the middle which is called optimal arousal or calm/organized alert.

The arousal bar

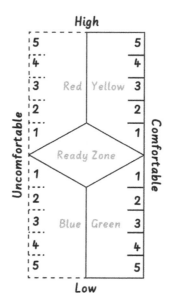

This book will use the **arousal bar** to represent changing states of arousal. When working with children, the term energy bar is often easier for them to understand. On the arousal bar, the vertical sections on the bar represent high, middle and low levels of arousal or energy. The diamond in the middle represents what I like to call the Ready Zone. This is a balanced state of arousal where energy is not too high or too low. It is sometimes called the 'just right' level of arousal.

To be able to learn and attend, the brain and body need to have the right level of arousal for the task. If arousal is **too high**, then the thinking parts of the brain can't process information effectively. For example, if you have a fear of spiders and there is a spider in your classroom, your arousal will be far too high to do any learning (or teaching!).

If arousal is **too low**, then the brain will not have sufficient focus and attention to learn. This is what happens to most of us at the end of a long day of training, we struggle to take information in as our brains are tired and we can't focus anymore!

Note from Kim

It is important to ensure that children know that **all arousal states are okay**. When starting out with regulation activities, unfortunately there can sometimes be a focus on being 'calm' all the time. Other arousal states are seen as 'bad'. This should never be the focus. **Different arousal states would be expected in different situations.** If a child is hurt or worried or about to do something exciting, their arousal will likely be higher. This would be expected and is normal. Children should learn that all arousal states are okay. They also must learn that it is important to keep themselves and others safe. This is where strategies can help.

Arousal and attention

Arousal is different from attention. Arousal refers to the level of energy and alertness in the body, whereas **attention** is the **cognitive process of concentrating on specific information**. The two processes are separate, but they work alongside each other.

Our level of arousal impacts our ability to pay attention. For example, if you are really tired, it's hard to pay attention. Equally if your arousal is high, because you are stressed about something, it will be harder for you to sustain your attention on something else.

In addition, something you are paying attention to can increase or decrease your arousal. For example, if a bee flies into your personal space, you will likely pay attention to it, and it will increase your arousal. Your brain will likely continue to pay attention to the bee until it is a safe distance away. At this time, you will stop listening to the information your friend is trying to tell you as your attention is focused on the bee! Your arousal will also have increased as your brain has perceived the bee as a potential threat.

Factors that impact arousal level

There are many things that impact our level of arousal. Many of these parallel Maslow's Hierarchy of Needs (Maslow 1943). To be in an optimal state of arousal, basic needs must be met first. For example, if you really need to go to the toilet, you will struggle to focus on a film (or your teacher). Both internal and external sensations impact arousal. Current and historical events also impact our current state of arousal.

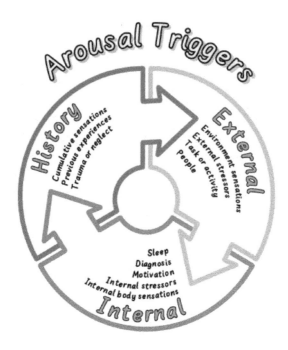

INTERNAL FACTORS

- **Internal body sensations:** Remember, this is called interoception. Hunger, needing the toilet, illness and pain will impact the attention the brain can give to other activities.

- **Sleep:** Great sleep or lack of sleep has a significant impact on arousal. When an individual is tired, their arousal is often lower. High arousal levels can also impact sleep, for example when stressed a person may find it harder to get to sleep. This is unfortunately often a vicious cycle whereby not sleeping increases stress, which makes it even harder to sleep.

- **Internal stressors:** These are the stressors that individuals put on themselves, such as reaching a certain grade or quality of work. These differ from the external standards set by others; they are the internal standards or expectations that we set ourselves.

- **Motivation:** The child's motivation to complete the activity impacts their arousal level. If they are excited or worried about the activity, their arousal will likely increase.

- **Diagnosis:** If the child has a specific diagnosis (e.g., autism, Down's syndrome, or specific language disorder) this can impact their capacity and ability to process sensory information and stay regulated. The child's communication skills must be considered here too.

EXTERNAL FACTORS

- **Environment sensations:** Every environment has specific sensory inputs. These will impact an individual's arousal. Some children may find a sporting stadium too overwhelming, whereas others might love the energy and noise.

- **People:** It is important to remember that there are also people in the child's environment. Relationships with different people impact arousal and subsequently performance. Most children freeze and modify their behaviour when the headteacher or principal walks into the room. This is often an inhibition of high arousal by part of the brain, and it is directly related to the person in the room.

- **Task or activity:** The activity the child is doing needs to be considered. If it is a task the child finds easy or they are very familiar with, they will likely remain calm. However, if it's a more difficult, higher-stakes or unfamiliar task, arousal might increase. A perfect example of this is exam time. For some students, the exam conditions increase their arousal level, and this affects their performance. Dyspraxia can also impact arousal and behaviour. Not knowing how to plan or do an activity is stressful!

- **External stressors:** These are the stressors put onto an individual by other people or circumstances. A deadline or due date is an external stressor. An expectation from another person could also be an external stressor.

HISTORY

- **Cumulative sensations:** Arousal builds up over time, which means each sensation and experience builds onto the next. So, a child with sensitivities might be able to manage a sensory input for short periods, but over time their arousal will increase. Some children might be able to manage and hold themselves together in one situation, such as assembly, but this could lead to a meltdown or shut down afterwards, if they have not been given time and space to decrease their arousal level. If children are slower to process sensory inputs, their arousal might take longer to increase compared to their peers. So, their brains might only get going part way through a PE lesson, as they need the extra movement to increase their arousal.

- **Previous experiences:** A positive or negative experience historically will impact arousal. If the last time a child went to a theme park they were sick when they went on the rollercoaster, they will likely be far less excited to go again. But if they had a great time, their arousal will likely be higher as they will be excited to go again.

- **Trauma or neglect:** A final thing to consider is any trauma experiences the individual may have had. Trauma wires the brain in a different way. This means that individuals might be hyper alert to potential threats, even in safe environments. Or they may be used to shutting down in order to protect themselves. If a child you are supporting has a history of trauma, advice from trained professionals will help you to understand how their trauma history impacts on their present arousal.

Practical example

I remember working with one child who was **making great progress**. His mother was using the supports I had suggested, and he was responding positively. She came into our session one day reporting that the last few days had been a total disaster. His behaviour was almost worse than before we had started sessions. I asked if he was unwell, and she said no.

A few days later, I received an email from her suggesting that I had a 'crystal ball'. Her son came down with a **high temperature** and was **very unwell** the evening after I saw them. Once he was well again, his progress resumed. I find that **illness has a significant impact on the regulation** of children with sensory differences. Often, due to poor interoceptive awareness, they don't recognize the subtle changes in their body. It's important to consider these internal factors when you observe an unexpected change in behaviour.

Learn more

The following books explore different elements of the above concepts:

- Stress: *The Stress Solution* by Dr Rangan Chatterjee (2018, Penguin Life)

- Sleep: *Why We Sleep* by Matthew Walker (2017, Scribner)

- Trauma: *The Body Keeps the Score: Brain, Mind and Body in the Healing of Trauma* by Bessel van der Kolk (2014, Penguin Publishing Group)

Reflective practice

Let's consider how your arousal has impacted your performance in the following examples:

- Think of a time where an internal factor impacted your arousal. What was it and how did it impact your performance?

- How about a time when an external factor impacted your arousal and performance?

- Can you think of a time where historical events impacted your arousal level going into a situation?

Task and environment expectations

It is important to note that there is **no perfect single level of arousal which meets every situation**. In some environments, for example a library or cinema, it is expected that you will be quiet. However, in other environments, for example a sporting match or playground, it is expected that you will be much louder and engaged. **Each environment has its own expectations and demands.**

Tasks also require **different levels of arousal**. If you're trying to get a baby to sleep, you will lower your level of arousal to help them sleep. You might sing a lullaby, but you wouldn't start blaring loud music at them.

When playing a game of football, arousal levels need to be much higher to stay focused and to keep up with the speed of the game.

Throughout the day, week and month, every individual needs to **adjust their level of arousal to match the environment and task**. This adjustment is called regulation, and sometimes it's called homeostasis. Some children, particularly those with sensory differences or emotional immaturity, find this harder to do than others. They often need more support to find and stay in the Ready Zone.

Note from Kim

Different environments, situations and activities have different expected levels of arousal. For example, higher arousal would be expected if you were at a theme park and lower arousal would be normal at the end of your trip! **Arousal should fluctuate and change** through the day and in different situations. We need to be able to adjust to these changes in a way that matches the changing demands.

Arousal over time

It is normal for arousal to fluctuate across the day, week, month and year. Any teacher reading this will know that towards the end of term their arousal is much lower than at the start! Across a typical day, arousal will change depending on the time and the circumstances.

Let's look at Nicki's Monday. Nicki wakes up reasonably focused and attentive. She gets herself ready and then wakes up her children. As the children are getting dressed, she sorts out breakfast. Her son sits down to breakfast and knocks over his glass of milk. This increases Nicki's arousal, as she is already short of time and now must clean up the milk, which is on the floor. Her arousal stays high until she reaches the office, after getting her children to school on time, just! Her morning is uneventful at work. She experiences a dip in her arousal before lunch as she is getting hungry and a bit restless.

After eating and going for a brisk walk, Nicki's arousal is back on track to clear her inbox. She completes this quickly, until an email from her manager highlights that a Friday deadline has moved to Wednesday. Her arousal increases, as she knows that it is going to be difficult to get the work completed in two days instead of four. She speaks to her colleagues, and shares out the work, which helps to reduce her arousal level, and she heads off to pick up the kids.

After school, Nicki's arousal level usually increases. There are so many things to fit in before bedtime. Once the kids are in bed her arousal drops off, as she is tired. She puts on a quick load of laundry and asks her partner to hang it out, before heading off to bed. Through Nicki's day there were external and internal events that impacted her level of arousal.

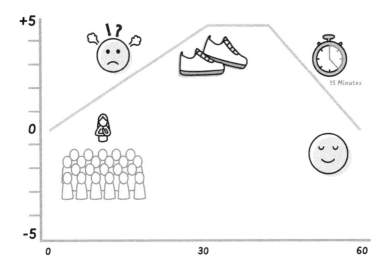

Reflective practice

Think about your own arousal across the day and week.

- When are your levels of arousal and attention at their best?
- When do they dip?
- What factors impact your own level of arousal?
- How do you think your level of arousal impacts the children in your classroom?

Neurology of arousal

When understanding arousal, it can be helpful to understand three main areas of the brain: the brain stem, the limbic system and the cortex. I like to think of them as the snake brain, the rat brain and the thinking brain. As humans have evolved from reptiles, our brain structure has become increasingly more complex.

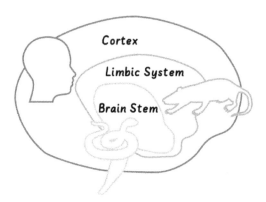

Brain stem

The **brain stem** is at the bottom of the brain. Its primary focus is survival. It controls basic body functions like breathing, heartbeat, digestion and urination. Hunger, thirst and sleep are also managed in part by the brain stem. There are some reflexive movements which it also controls, like blinking. I call the brain stem the **snake brain** because it is the one structure of our brain that we share with reptiles.

Limbic system

The **limbic system** is the next layer. In evolution, this developed on top of the brain stem. It is often called the 'old mammalian brain' as it was a change to the brain that occurred when mammals evolved. I call it the **rat brain** as this is easier to remember!

This part of our brain is primarily focused on **protection**. Its primary job is to **keep us safe**. The limbic system decides how important a sensory message is and how much attention needs to be paid to it. **Sensory responsivity**, or modulation, is organized here. In addition, the limbic system plays a huge role in **emotional responses** and creating memories.

This part of our brain initiates the **fight, flight, freeze response**. This is a safety response which we don't have conscious control over. For example, if you run into a spider's web, you might have the following reactions:

- You also swipe the air with your hand to push the spider's web away – you have initiated a **fight** response.

- You jump back and out of it – that's a **flight** response.

- You may panic and freeze, staying stuck in the web – that's a freeze response.

These responses happen **before you have time to think about them**. The limbic system notices the light touch of the spider's web. It identifies it as a potential threat and takes immediate action to keep the body safe.

Some children have this **automatic response to certain sensory inputs**. A child who runs away when the playtime whistle is blown is having a flight response to the whistle noise. It is important to understand that these **reactions are an automatic nervous system response**, rather than a conscious choice.

Cortex

The **cortex** is where our conscious thinking occurs. It is the size of our cortex that separates humans from other mammals. Our cortex supports planning and inhibition. It is responsible for **sensory discrimination, coordinated movement, and language**. I like to call it the **thinking brain** as it's where we do our more complicated thinking. It is this section of the brain that supports **learning at school**.

The cortex has some **control over the limbic system and brain stem**. For example, if the brain stem notifies the cortex that the body needs to urinate, the cortex can stop this from happening until we make it to the bathroom. However, if we ignore that sensation for too long, the brain stem takes back control, as it knows that holding on for too long is not safe, and the bladder can only hold a certain amount!

When we are under- or over-aroused, it can be difficult to access our cortex. This is why children (and adults) lose their language at times of high stress. Their limbic system is calling the shots and its primary focus is safety, not an in-depth conversation! This is why we make less rational decisions when we are stressed. The cortex is less responsive and less engaged.

Arousal and the brain

Arousal is a neurological process controlled by our brain. It is primarily controlled by a specific part of our nervous system called the **autonomic nervous system (ANS)**. The ANS is controlled by the brain stem and limbic system, or the snake brain and rat brain.

The ANS is designed to respond to threats in the environment and to relax when there are no threats. It changes our breathing, heart rate, blood circulation and digestion to match the level of safety it perceives we currently have. When a threat is high, it is the part of our nervous system that triggers a fight/flight/freeze response. In early human evolution, it was responsible for helping us to run away from predators. Nowadays it is triggered by far less severe threats, a work deadline for example, but the neurological response in our body is the same.

Arousal and learning

In order to learn in school, children need to be able to **access their cortex**, or thinking brain. This is where all higher-level conscious human thinking happens. To access thinking brain, the child's **arousal needs to be at the right level** (or in the Ready Zone).

Have you ever had a conversation with someone **when you were stressed**, then immediately forgotten the important piece of information that they told you? This is a perfect example of **arousal level impacting on learning and retention**. You forgot the information because your brain was stressed, your arousal was too high, and you couldn't access your thinking brain to process the information effectively.

Learning in school follows the same principle. **If a child's arousal is too high, or too low, they won't be able to process information effectively.** To learn successfully, arousal levels need to be right. Sensory strategies are one way to help to support arousal levels, but you must also consider all of the other things that might be impacting a child's level of arousal which we explored earlier in this chapter.

Note from Kim

Attention requires access to a part of the thinking brain called the pre-frontal cortex. **The brain will prioritize attention to threats first**, so a spider will gain a child's attention before their teacher. The brain also **pays attention to new stimuli** because it is trying to determine whether this is a threat or not. Threats and potential or perceived threats will always trump learning; this is particularly important to remember for children who have experienced trauma or neglect.

Learn more

There are numerous books which explore the brain's neurology. One that is very accessible and considers the impact of the brain's chemistry on our daily lives is *How to Have a Good Day* by Caroline Webb (2016, Macmillan). *The Whole-Brain Child* by Daniel Siegel and Tina Payne Bryson (2012, Robinson) is another example.

Note from Kim

This representation is **extremely simplistic**. The brain is a highly connected mass of cells. It contains **80+ billion neurons**, the cells which make up the brain. Each of these can create 10,000+ connections with other neurons. There is also another area called the cerebellum which fine tunes our movement. It is completely beyond the scope of this book to describe the brain in detail. My goal is to give you a brief overview, but I hope this overview gives you a basic understanding of why children may respond in the way they do.

Reflective practice

Can you think of a time when your rat brain took over? It happens to everyone. Think about what led up to the situation and how you reacted. What would you have done differently if your thinking brain was in control?

Overload and shut down

Sensory overload is a term used to describe the response which occurs when a child has received **too much sensory information**. It is commonly reported by those who experience over-responsivity (hyper-reactivity) and by autistic individuals. Sensory overload is essentially a **fight, flight, freeze response**. It is the brain trying to protect itself as there is just too much for it to process.

Shut down is another term which is frequently used. This is a freeze response in relation to sensory overload. The brain shuts down in order to **protect itself and to be able to manage in the situation**. The child may be unresponsive. When this occurs, the child will need time and access to a space or strategy that helps them to calm down.

Note from Kim

Overload and shut down can **sometimes look like low arousal**. However, when they occur, the **child's arousal is in fact too high**. This means that you need to use sensory supports to help them to lower their arousal. If you use alerting strategies, you will overload the child further. We will explore this in more detail in the next chapter.

Regulation

Regulation is the **ability to adjust and change your level of arousal to match the demands of a task and the environment**. For example, if you are running late, your arousal will increase due to stress. Once you reach your destination the brain should lower your arousal and help you to recover. The brain is constantly regulating your state of arousal throughout the day, often unconsciously.

Humans **can consciously regulate** their arousal level if required. We do this by increasing or decreasing our arousal to match demands. For example, we can remain calm when a toddler is having a tantrum, or at work if someone is arguing with us. We have greater capacity to do this when our level of arousal is in an optimal state (or when we are in the Ready Zone!).

Sometimes, **specific circumstances will dictate the level of arousal required** and we can adjust to this. For example, if you knew your friend had just received some very bad news, you would likely adjust your greeting to be less jovial than it ordinarily might be. You regulate your level of arousal to match the specific circumstance. Some people are more skilled at this than others.

When there are **sensory responsivity differences**, regulation can be even more challenging. This is because the child's nervous system processes sensory inputs with different levels of intensity. A child who is over-responsive, and has sensitivity to sensory information, will need to work much harder to lower their arousal in environments where they experience sensory overload. A child who is slower to process sensory information usually needs to work harder to increase their arousal to the level that is required for the task.

Isla's arousal – over-responsivity (sensitivity)

Isla is a six-year-old autistic girl. She experiences sound and touch sensitivities. At school, she finds it difficult to block out the whirring of the projector and the ticking of the clock. These background noises increase her level of arousal throughout the day. She must work harder to calm her body down (decrease her arousal) and focus on her teacher. The PE hall is extremely hard for her to stay calm in because the sounds echo and significantly increase her level of arousal. She never engages in messy play and dislikes art because of the sticky textures like glue and tape. She struggles with certain clothing fabrics, including her school uniform. Sensory strategies could be used in this case to help her to lower her arousal level and avoid sensory overload.

Noah's arousal – slower responses

Noah is an eight-year-old boy with Down's syndrome. His vestibular and proprioceptive senses are slower to respond (hypo-reactive). He really struggles to stay seated at his desk all day and often leans over or is slumped. He also finds it tricky to keep focused on what his teacher is saying when she talks for long periods. He gets tired in the afternoon. In PE, he finds it hard to keep up with the other children and his balance is poor. Sensory strategies could be used with Noah to help to increase his level of arousal. He also experiences sound sensitivity, and this must be considered when creating his sensory plan.

Note from Kim

Another term I will use in the following sections is '**dysregulated**'. Dysregulated is the **opposite of regulated**. What is important to remember is that this doesn't always mean that their arousal is too high. Often, we think of dysregulation as angry or out-of-control behaviour, but it's important to remember that an individual may freeze or dissociate. These responses are also indicators of dysregulation and that an individual's arousal is not in a balanced state.

Development of regulation

Regulation **develops over time and with experiences**. The process starts when children are babies. Long before they can self-regulate, they need help from their caregivers. This is called **co-regulation**. When babies start to show distress, their caregivers swaddle, carry, rock and feed them. As their needs are met, the infant learns patterns and rhythms. They learn that when they hear mum or dad's footsteps, help is on the way. By helping the baby to organize their arousal, caregivers are laying the foundations for self-regulation in the future.

Toddlers need huge amounts of support from their caregivers to **regulate and self-soothe**. While they are starting to be more independent, the regulation centres of their brain continue to develop. Parenting expert Sarah Ockwell-Smith (2015) notes that it isn't until **after a child's fifth birthday that their brain is developmentally mature enough for them to start to self-soothe or self-regulate**. Parents of teenagers would also argue that hormones can severely disrupt this skill.

Co-regulation

Regulation starts with **co-regulation**, or **someone else helping the child to regulate**. While we are focused on children, it is helpful to remember that adults help adults to regulate all the time. Think about when a friend or family member was upset, and you gave them a hug. Or a time when they were angry, and you listened and helped them to calm down.

Regulation through the help of caregivers is what teaches children to self-regulate as they get older. They learn what they experience. Co-regulation helps them to develop the brain networks and strategies they need to self-regulate.

Learn more

When there is trauma and neglect, children typically have not experienced supportive co-regulation historically. This impacts the development of their brain and means that their brain connections are not mature. These children will need additional support to learn to self-regulate. This interview with Oprah Winfrey and Dr Bruce Perry explores the links between trauma and brain development: www.youtube.com/watch?v=uUAL8RVvkyY (available from SXSW EDU). They explore the topic further in the book *What Happened to You? Conversations on Trauma, Resilience and Healing* (2021, Flatiron Books).

Self-regulation

Self-regulation is the ability to **stay regulated without the help of others**. It is the ability to use strategies independently to either calm down or energize yourself. Neurodiverse children (and adults) often need more support to learn self-regulation. Sensory strategies are one tool that can be used to help.

Each time a child **experiences dysregulation and successfully re-regulates**, they learn what strategies help them. This **strengthens the connections** between the limbic system and the cortex and **gives them more awareness** and control of their level of arousal in the future. Over time, they can successfully self-regulate, but it **starts with co-regulation**. There will also be times when their arousal has reached an extreme level and they need additional support again. It's the adult's job to support the child until they can self-regulate.

PRACTICAL APPLICATION

It is important to remember that children **shouldn't be expected to self-regulate until they can co-regulate successfully**. I have seen many examples when a child has been told to just 'calm down' or they have been sent to use a sensory strategy by themselves. **Some children will need explicit teaching to use sensory supports.** You need to ensure they can use the strategies successfully with you there first before you expect them to use them independently.

Note from Kim

Children with **attachment issues** will need a lot more co-regulation initially as strong attachment in relationships is what will help them to self-regulate in the future. Sometimes these children will **deliberately sabotage** efforts to regulate because **they need the adult connection**, and they know that once they are 'calm' the adult will direct their attention elsewhere. **Strong attachment relationships** will support these children to self-regulate over time, but they must start with co-regulation and trust.

Emotional regulation

Emotional regulation refers to the **ability to regulate our emotional responses**. Toddlers and teenagers find this difficult. For toddlers, this is because they haven't yet established the language and brain connections to enable them to regulate their emotions. Teenagers find this more difficult as their hormones and brain connections are changing. They need time to get used to these changes.

Neurologically, the front part of our cortex (specifically the frontal lobe) is responsible for emotional regulation. The connections from the limbic system to this part of the brain continue to develop into adulthood. The ability to regulate emotions improves as these connections strengthen. Again, some individuals need more support to develop these skills. This is particularly true when there are social, communication or language difficulties (e.g., autism, developmental language disorder).

Interoception supports regulation

To be able to self-regulate, first we need **good awareness of the internal messages coming from our body**. These messages indicate that our arousal level is changing. We need to recognize if our heart rate or breathing has increased. We need to identify when we are hungry. We need to know if we have enough energy to focus on an activity. This internal awareness is the first step in choosing a support strategy.

The earlier we can identify, or feel, changes to our arousal level, or where we are on the arousal bar, **the easier it is to change it**. It is much easier to calm down from a Red 2 than it is from a Red 5. Children who are not recognizing internal state shifts early are often the ones who appear to 'explode out of nowhere'. **Very rarely is this explosion out of nowhere**, it is just that the child (and potentially those around them) has not recognized the earlier signs of dysregulation.

There are three key things (Goodall 2021) the child needs to be aware of:

- Their own internal body state.

- Their own feelings and emotions.

- The impact of external stimulation.

We will explore these further in Chapter 6.

Teacher perspective – Dr Emma Goodall

Teachers need students to be in the 'Ready Zone' to be able to learn. Some students are able to regulate themselves from quite a young age, while others struggle with self-regulation all the way through secondary school. It can be difficult for teachers to work out when students are being naughty and when they are unable to manage their emotions or behaviour. However, it is really important to be able to make that distinction, particularly around students' interoception.

When students are overloaded and in that fight, flight or freeze zone (survival mode), they cannot learn as their brain and body are literally focused on surviving. If they were being chased by a crocodile, this would be an appropriate biological response. However, it is not so appropriate when they are not able to differentiate between a truly threatening context and one that is not, such as someone being too close to them in assembly. In school, this might look like a student running out of assembly (flight) and then hitting the teaching assistant who goes to check they are okay (fight). It can also look like a student hiding under a desk or trashing the room. The brain can take at least 15 minutes to calm down once the student starts to de-escalate. However, teachers are powerless to help, except by keeping everyone away and minimizing sensory input for the student, until the young person is no longer in survival mode.

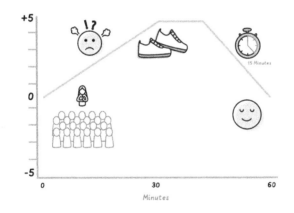

When students are not given enough time to neurologically calm down they often arc up again within a short space of time and quickly earn a reputation for being dysregulated most of the time. A key sensory factor impacting regulation is the student's interoceptive awareness. If a student has low levels of interoception they will not be aware when they are becoming stressed or distressed, only possibly noticing when they are experiencing difficult emotions once the emotions are really intense and controlling them rather than them controlling the emotions. In the classroom, these students often appear to be fine unless they totally explode with rage or implode with extreme distress. When this occurs, the teacher quite reasonably may assume that the trigger was the last thing that happened or was said, when in reality the student's feelings may have been building up for hours or days or even weeks and the 'perceived trigger' was merely the proverbial straw that broke the camel's back. Supporting students to develop their interoception will over time enable them to notice and then manage their emotions and feelings more easily and effectively (Goodall 2021; Goodall & Brownlow 2022).

Sensory seeking to regulate

Sometimes children will be **actively trying to self-regulate** using one of their senses. At first glance, these children will appear to be seeking additional sensory input. However, when you observe further you will see that they *are* actively trying to self-regulate.

A common example of this is **chewing**. At first glance, the child appears to be 'seeking proprioceptive sensory input'. This is a correct observation, but further analysis might identify that the child is seeking out the proprioceptive sensory input because it is calming. They will most likely be using this input to try to dampen down the impact of sensitivities with other senses (e.g., noise) and avoid sensory overload.

Making sounds is another good example. Some children with sensitivity to sounds will make their own sounds. They do this to drown out or cover up other sounds in the environment. For example, I worked with one boy who would scream when he tipped the Lego box onto the floor. He found the sound of the bricks tumbling out overwhelming, and his scream was his way of drowning it out.

Sensory processing is much more complicated than it may first seem. **The more you understand, the more you notice.** The more you start observing sensory patterns, the more skilled you will become at separating out these nuisances.

Stimming

Stimming is the name that is given to **repetitive movements or actions which autistic children make**. Common stims include hand flapping, looking persistently out of the corners of the eye, watching spinning objects, and jumping. Some children may also have vocal stims where they repeat phrases or sounds.

Sensory stims typically occur for three reasons:

1. **Regulation:** The child has learned that the stim helps them to regulate, so they do it at times when their arousal is too high, or too low.

2. **Enjoyment:** Many children love the sensation of their stim, so they choose to do it.

3. **Boredom:** Dyspraxia often occurs alongside autism and sometimes children don't have an idea for play or can't independently self-occupy, so the sensory stim is a way to occupy time or play as it's something they enjoy.

Historically, there was a huge push to stop stimming. However, conventional thinking identifies that **sensory stims can be very helpful for the child**, especially if they are using them to regulate. Often when there is an expectation that the child doesn't do their stim, they **spend all their brain power inhibiting their stim**. This means they aren't accessing learning. The other thing that can happen when a child is **expected to stop a stim** is that they will **develop another one**, which may not be as safe or as helpful for them.

When to stop a sensory stim

There are two times when adapting or stopping a sensory stim should be considered.

The first is if it is **unsafe**. For example, some children will head bang into a hard surface. This stim is unsafe and should be adapted. Can they be redirected to head bang into a cushion or beanbag? Or can the movement be provided by a rocking chair or rocking horse? When providing an alternative, it should **still target the sense the child is seeking out**. So, a weighted blanket (touch pressure/proprioception) would probably not be an appropriate alternative for rocking (vestibular) as it **doesn't** target the same sense.

The second time a stim should be redirected is if the child is doing the stim at the **expense of all other activities or engagement**. In this case, the first thing you need to consider is what in the environment and task is overloading the child. These changes or supports need to be in place first. Then, an approach which considers joint attention and engagement is recommended, such as Intensive Interaction, Floortime, Attention Autism and Ayres® Sensory Integration Therapy. When children have reasonable understanding, a now/next board may also be helpful.

Learn more

To really understand why stopping stims is unhelpful, watch the videos on my website. In the article, I explore why stopping sensory stimming should never be the target goal. There are also videos where autistic adults explore their experiences: www.griffinot.com/ how-to-stop-child-sensory-stimming.

The goal of sensory strategies

There are **two goals in using sensory strategies**. The first is to support the child to **maintain the level of arousal** they need to participate in an environment or activity. The second is to **support regulation**, so that the child does not become under- or over-aroused. You might be working on both goals at the same time, but at the end of the day you are **supporting a child to match their arousal to the activity and environment**.

An understanding of the senses helps you to **know which sensation** might be triggering the response. Awareness of the sensory response types helps you to **understand why** a student might be responding in a certain way to sensations. Knowledge of arousal and regulation helps you to see when a student might need additional supports. Combining this information will help you to use sensory supports successfully to allow children to participate, engage and learn.

Reflective practice

Think about your own experiences using sensory strategies.

- ◆ Have you used them before?

- ◆ What were your goals for using them? (Did you set any?)

Chapter 3

Evaluation and Goal Setting

'Evaluation, goal setting and monitoring are key to ensuring success with sensory strategies.'

The goal of using sensory strategies is to support regulation and participation. **Before** creating a plan, it is important to evaluate the child's needs. It is important to **consider the whole child**, rather than just their sensory needs. This includes the **underlying factors** impacting their overall arousal. The chapter will explore tools you can use to review behaviours. It will also discuss sensory assessment, checklists and screens.

Identifying individual needs

The first step when using sensory strategies is to identify the **individual needs that require support**. In a classroom of 30 children, it is highly likely that at least two children will have some differences in processing the sensations occurring in the room. If you have an autistic child in your class, it is highly probable that they will experience some differences when processing sensory messages. It is highly **unlikely** that these children will all have the same sensory profile and response patterns!

Before you start using sensory supports, you need some **baseline information to help you** to understand the individual's sensory preferences. Certain sensory supports will help multiple children in your class; for example, reducing the visual distractions on displays could be helpful for many children.

Start with strengths

Historically, there has been a huge focus on what a child can't do. What are their weaknesses? Weaknesses were used to identify relevant supports. This is slowly changing to a focus on strengths-based assessment.

Strengths-based assessment flips the narrative. Instead of starting with weaknesses, we look at strengths and **use these strengths to help to support other areas**. For sensory needs, this means starting with the environment or task where the child is successful, rather than one where they are struggling.

When the child is successful, what is it about the environment or task? How is it meeting their sensory needs or preferences? What qualities are allowing the child to experience success? What is it about the environmental setup? Don't forget to consider the adults and children in the space! What did the child do before they started? The qualities of the space and task can be used to understand what supports will help the child.

Starting with success gives you a framework to understand what needs to be adapted or changed in environments where the child is unsuccessful. For example, if the child was successful in one classroom but not another, what is it that changed? What can be moved to the current classroom as a support? Or, if they are successful at home and not school, what is different? While not everything at home can be implemented at school, there are likely to be some things that can be integrated.

Teacher perspective – Dr Emma Goodall

Many education systems and individual schools have moved away from deficit-based thinking to strengths-based planning. That said, **funding can still be very much viewed as only being possible through using deficit-based language**. Unfortunately, this can colour the way teachers understand sensory differences. For autistic students, sensory differences can be a source of calm or even joy and are often described as sensory stims. Examples can be tapping the table, running sand through fingers, running hands over the carpet or listening to the same piece of music over and over.

Children and young people themselves are the best source of information about their sensory likes and dislikes, followed by their families and support team. However, observations of students will also provide a wealth of information when done with an open mind and active thinking about external and internal sensory things that students may be experiencing atypically.

For example, observing in a classroom, it might be seen that one student is agitated when sitting under the air conditioner, and focused when sitting far away from it. Unless the teacher is actively thinking about sensory challenges, they may not even take the air conditioner into account, instead focusing on who the student is sitting next to.

Students who have **poor proprioception** can be described as clumsy, which implies they are deliberately bumping into people and furniture. In fact, they do not know where their bodies end and space begins, which means they misjudge distances and may struggle with depth perception; in the classroom this looks like walking straight into people and tripping over their own feet. This is not fun for anyone, least of all the student themselves. For some students, wearing gloves can help them know where the tips of their hands are, making them less likely to accidentally whack people as they are walking past!

Where a student has an **occupational therapist** in their support team, they will be an invaluable support for teachers learning to identify and understand the sensory profile of that student and how to support them as effectively as possible within the constraints of school.

Note from Kim

It can also be **more inclusive to make supports available to all children in the classroom**. Initially, most children will test everything. However, over time they will identify what helps them, and what doesn't. Usually, they will then choose the supports that help. If children are not using supports correctly, sensory passports (see end of chapter) can help them to understand what supports are most beneficial for them.

Factors that impact arousal

In Chapter 2, we explored the factors that impact arousal. It is important to include these in your evaluation, as they will impact the child's responses. If you are observing different responses at different times, it may be because of one of these factors. You should already have a reasonable understanding of most of these factors. The environment and the task demands will be explored further.

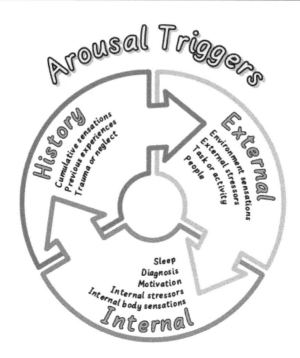

Environment

It is helpful to consider the **impact of each environment the child must participate in**. In **primary school** there is typically one main classroom, but there are usually a few specialist classrooms (e.g., music, PE hall). The child will also be in a different space for break and lunchtimes. Their arousal could be different in these different environments.

If you are a **secondary school** teacher, the environment is very different. The child needs to transition frequently through the day. Each classroom is different. Most sensory equipment is not suitable because it is too big to move around the school. Many strategies may not be appropriate because of space and time constraints.

Another thing that changes in different environments are the **adults**. It is important that we consider the impact that different adults may have. Temporary staff need to be provided with relevant information so they too can help to support the children to be successful.

Task demands and structure

It is important to think about the impact that **task demands have on children's ability and anxiety**. This includes the language, planning and physical demands. Sometimes a child's arousal will increase because they find the task difficult. Other tasks might decrease their arousal (think about how a three-hour Zoom training impacts your focus and attention).

If a child has **language processing difficulties or poor planning or organization** (e.g., dyspraxia/DCD), this will impact their behaviour. Not every behaviour response is due to sensory responsivity. Sometimes, it is just that **the task demands are too high (or too low) for the child**. The child's diagnosis and developmental ability need to be considered in your evaluation of the task.

The structure of the task will also impact on arousal. Some children find free choice/free flow play activities (including lunchtime) easier because they are not constrained and do not have to participate in activities that overload their senses. Other children find this much harder potentially because they can't come up with a plan of what to do, or because there are extra noises and visual sensory inputs with the other children moving around.

Reflective practice

Can you think about an example of when an environment or specific task has affected your own arousal?

Learn more

The book *Why Zebras Don't Get Ulcers* by Robert Sapolsky (2004, Holt Paperbacks) considers how our lifestyle impacts our arousal and stress levels.

Behaviour observations

When trying to understand behaviours, it is **helpful to observe behaviour over time**. This helps you to consider triggers and how consequences impact behaviour. Sometimes, there will be a sensory trigger, but this is not always the case. Sometimes, it's **communication difficulties** that trigger the behaviour. Sometimes, the behaviour is driven by another need such as **pain**, or **attachment issues**. Some children will just be **testing boundaries**, especially if they are working at a two- to three-year-old level.

It can be helpful to **observe the incident multiple times**. This lets you consider all elements. Using a **dated chart** or diary format can help you to identify patterns. For example, a diary may show that the child always struggles on Tuesday. This **pattern** might help you to realize that the music lesson which happens on Tuesday is a trigger for that child. It's important to consider all the factors outlined in Chapter 2 when reviewing triggers and outcomes.

In addition, it is incredibly important to consider **how consequences might reinforce behaviours**. Sometimes what is perceived to be a consequence by the adult **isn't perceived in the same way** by the child. One example is missing out on playtime; some children prefer to sit and read rather than be out on the playground.

Another example is sending a child to a separate room if they hit another student. If the child hit out because they were overloaded, they **might perceive the punishment** of being sent to an isolated space **as a reward**. The isolated space will be a quiet space which allows them to regulate and is supportive to their nervous system. If they **don't have another way to request this** when they are overloaded, they may start to hit out in order to be sent to a quiet space!

If you need to **structure your observations**, the ABC and STAR models can help with analysis. You can use the information gathered to consider what triggered the behaviour/s and what changes you could make to support the child. It is helpful to start with the facts and specific observations, before thinking about the reasons behind the behaviour; for example, recording that the child was rocking back and forth, rather than 'seeking vestibular input'. Write down what you see first.

ABC

The ABC model considers what happened before and after the behaviour. There are three sections:

1. **A**ntecedent: What happened before the behaviour occurred? What was the trigger? Think about the environment, task and people in the space. Make sure you consider the adult's actions as well as the child's.

2. **B**ehaviour: What was the observable behaviour? What did the behaviour look like? Who was involved, both children and adults? How long did the behaviour continue for?

3. **C**onsequence: What happened afterwards? Consider what

the child and adult did. What were their reactions? Where did the child go afterwards? What activities did they get to do? Consider if this consequence was perceived as a consequence, or a reward, by the child.

STAR

The STAR model is very similar to the ABC model; however, it breaks the observations down under different headings.

1. **S**etting: The environment or where the behaviour happened. Make sure you consider the space, people and task.

2. **T**rigger: What triggered the behaviour? Consider sensory inputs, time of day, activity and interactions with others. Was there something you could see that directly led to the child's behaviour? Sometimes this can be the absence of a staff member or routine. Sometimes it might be the behaviour of another child.

3. **A**ction: What behaviour occurred? What did the child do? Make sure you are specific when you describe the behaviour.

4. **R**esult: What was the consequence? This includes how others reacted. Sometimes, individuals with poor communication skills will repeat behaviours in order to receive a response or reaction. They may be trying to interact with their peers, but as they don't have language skills they might hit their peer because their peer pays attention to them when they are hit. And, as already mentioned, consider how the child perceives the consequence.

Practical example

In a special school I supported, one child had a significantly higher number of physical interventions on their behaviour record. This child often hit other children or staff. When they did this, they were held in a specific wrap.[1] Observing their behaviour over time, staff realized that the child was actively hitting other students when their arousal

---

1   Staff were Team Teach trained. Team Teach is an approach to supporting unsafe behaviour which includes specific physical holds. Staff must complete training before they use this intervention.

increased. Using the ABC approach, we hypothesized that they were seeking out the firm pressure, which the hold provided, as a regulation strategy.

The student had identified that the **firm pressure** (consequence) **helped to calm** them when their arousal increased (antecedent), but the **only way they knew how to request** this was to hit a peer (behaviour). We put in place a **communication card** which allowed the student to request a firm hold. Staff initially used the same hold they would for behaviour management, as they knew this regulated the student. Over time, they changed this to a variation of hugs, touch pressure and a weighted blanket. The ABC approach helped staff to really **analyse the situation and to make positive changes for the student**.

Sensory evaluation
Formal assessment tools
Occupational therapists and other health professionals often use assessment tools that **compare sensory processing to a 'typical' population**. These assessments give a score for sensory responsivity or motor skills. Some of the more commonly used ones which specifically assess sensory processing are:

- **Sensory Profile – 2 (SP2):** This tool is a parent and teacher questionnaire which considers sensory reactivity. It gives a score for each of the senses. It also gives a combined score for four reactivity quadrants: seeking, under-responsive, avoiding and sensitivity. This tool also considers behavioural responses that are not considered in the other tools.

- **Sensory Processing Measure – 2 (SPM2):** This tool is another parent and teacher questionnaire. It considers social skills, sensory reactivity and praxis. It gives separate scores for each sense, social skill and praxis, and a total score. The total scores don't consider whether the response is over- or under-reactive. The therapist will make a clinical judgement on the individual questions.

- **Sensory Integration and Praxis Test (SIPT):** This is the assessment tool developed by A. Jean Ayres. It primarily considers whether a child has dyspraxia or postural control challenges. It must be completed by a trained therapist. It is very dated, and is time consuming to complete and score. Many therapists will transition to the EASI when it is available.

- **Evaluation of Ayres Sensory Processing (EASI):** This is a new tool which considers both reactivity and motor skills. It has similar activities to the SIPT and must be completed by a trained therapist. At the time of writing, this tool was not published but is in the final stages of development.

- **Sensory Processing 3-Dimensions Scale (SP3D):** This is a new assessment which is being developed by Lucy Miller's team. It will use physical activities to assess for sensory modulation, discrimination and movement. At the time of writing, this tool was not yet published, but once it is you will see it mentioned in reports.

- **Clinical observations:** Therapists complete a group of movements and postures which are called 'clinical observations'. Many therapists use an informal checklist of the movements. These have been standardized in a new tool called the Structured Observations of Sensory Integration – Motor (SOSI-M).

Checklists

Many sensory books include checklists to help with identification of sensory differences. There are also checklists on websites. Some of these are written for the children rather than the adults around them. Three books with checklists are:

- *The Sensory Team Handbook* by Nancy Mucklow (2010). This book is written for slightly older children and teenagers. The questionnaires can be completed by the child and show patterns of under- or over-responsivity for each sense.

- *Sensory Perceptual Issues in Autism and Asperger Syndrome* by Olga Bogdashina (2003). A tool is available in this book. It is written specifically for autistic children. It is quite long. It considers responses for each sense and produces a visual representation of the total scores.

- *Sensational Kids: Hope and Help for Children with Sensory Processing Disorder (SPD)* by Lucy Miller (2014). This book includes checklists at the start of each chapter.

Screening tool

To help your understanding, there is **a screening tool included in the Appendix**. The tool considers common behaviours you might see for each response type. There also is a **pdf download** available you can use with your children in the **additional materials**. The tool also has been used to explore the sensory responses for the case studies at the end of the book.

There is a **table for each sense** which is broken into sensitivity, slow and seeking. Behaviours that may link to each response type are listed. There is also a box which lists indicators that the child might be using the sensory behaviour to help to regulate another sense. The tool is not specifically standardized and **should never be used to make a diagnosis**.

The screening tool is **designed to help you identify which senses the child might need more support with**. It also considers the other factors that might be impacting the child's ability to regulate. You can use the tool to **group sensory patterns**. You can then use these patterns to help to inform you which sensory supports might be best suited to the child's needs.

First, **tick or highlight the statements that are relevant to that child**. Then, look to see if one box has a lot more ticks than another. This will **indicate potential sensory reactivity patterns** and help you to know which strategies might be appropriate. In some cases, the tools will indicate difficulties in all areas. When this happens, you need to prioritize the senses that are having the most significant impact on the child's ability to participate.

Note from Kim

Behaviour can be a very unhelpful term. It is often used to describe negative behaviour. I used the term because it is common language. However, I ask that you pause for a moment when observing any behaviour and remember that **behaviour is always communication**. It might be that the child cannot verbally express their preference or needs so they respond by walking off. The task could be too hard. There may be underlying attachment insecurities or trauma experiences which shape the response you are seeing. It can also be a response to sensory inputs. Your job is to **investigate what the behaviour you are observing is actually communicating**. I promise there will always be a reason, even if that reason does not seem logical to you.

Setting individual goals

Once you have identified the child's sensory preferences and needs, you need to **consider the goal/s you have for using the sensory strategies with them**. What changes do you want to see? What activity or environment do you want them to be able to participate in? Do you want them to be able to increase or decrease their arousal? These goals can be recorded on your existing documentation or on a sensory passport (see the next page).

Example goals

- When using her weighted blanket and ear defenders, Isla will be able to sit and attend during assembly for 15 minutes.

- Noah will identify when he needs to increase his arousal during lessons. Noah will independently access the 'Move it Zone' to help himself to reorganize so he can complete his work.

Note from Kim

It is important that the end target of a goal is **not related to the removal of a sensory strategy** (for example, after eight weeks Tom will be able to focus without using his wobble cushion). It is best to consider sensory supports as you would a pair of glasses. **If they are working, they are supporting the child to participate**, in the same way glasses would allow them to see to read. You would never write a goal that suggested a child should be able to read without their glasses. Please think of sensory supports in the same way!

Recording and sensory passports

Each school will have their own recording systems. They will record incidents, behaviour observations and analysis, and this information should inform goal setting and strategies. **It can help if the student's goals, preferences, triggers and support strategies are listed clearly**

in one accessible place. This is especially helpful when multiple staff are supporting classes, and when staff are on leave. One way to pull this information together is in a sensory passport.

Sensory passport

A sensory passport is a short one- or two-page document that outlines the **student's goals, preferences, triggers, arousal state indicators and support strategies**. It should be a quick reference tool that staff can use. It should be stored in a clearly accessible place in every classroom, so that staff can find it easily. Sometimes it's helpful to have it up on the wall.

My name:		
My goals:		
My sensory preferences:		My sensory triggers:
My communication supports:		
My arousal		
Arousal	I look like	This helps
0		
Red 3		
Yellow 3		
Blue 3		
Green 3		
S = I can do this independently. **H** = I need help.		

The case studies in the Appendix both contain example sensory passports. This format is just one example, and maps to the arousal bar. You can adapt the passport to suit the regulation programme you use. It can be helpful to include the different levels of arousal, as often there are changes to behaviour which can be observed before a child becomes very dysregulated.

Note from Kim

This structure is just an example, and you can **adapt it to meet your school's needs**. If the student has supports in place for a variety of needs, a 'student passport' might be a more helpful name. While longer documentation is always required for the student's full file, it is highly recommended that their **passport is a maximum of two pages**. Ideally, it should only be one page. The idea of this document is that it's **a quick reference for staff to use daily**. New, temporary or cover staff can also use it to know immediately how to support the student. If it's too long, then it will not be a helpful document.

Monitoring impact

The final consideration, before choosing sensory supports, is deciding **how and when to monitor the impact**. Sensory supports should not just be put in place and left. The goals you have set, and the impact of the support, should be monitored. It is helpful to decide the frequency and structure of the monitoring before you start so that you have clear data.

Using goals to monitor progress

The student's goals are a good way to monitor progress. To do this, you must **collect baseline data before you start, to check what has changed**. Here's two examples using the goals above.

Isla

Goal: *When using her weighted blanket and ear defenders, Isla will be able to sit and attend during assembly for 15 minutes.*

Monitoring: *Record the amount of time Isla spends in assembly two weeks prior to using the sensory supports, then over time as she uses them. Plot the data into a graph to show progress (or to show no progress and indicate that a different strategy is required).*

Noah

Goals: *Noah will identify when he needs to increase his arousal during lessons. Noah will independently access the 'Move it Zone' to help himself to reorganize so that he can complete his work.*

Monitoring: *Record the number of times Noah's arousal decreased and* *the number of times he identified this. Record the number of times he went to the 'Move it Zone' and if this was independently or with support from an adult. Tracking this data over time will help to show you Noah's progress. It will also be important to track if the activities in the 'Move it Zone' helped him to reorganize.*

Using existing documentation

You can also use existing documentation within school to monitor progress. This could include:

- Behaviour incident charts/records

- Academic progress

- Attendance

- Parent feedback

- Staff feedback.

Reviewing incidents

If the child is making progress, but **then their behaviour changes**, it is important to go back to observations and analysis. Consider what changed for the child at home and at school. It might be that the child is sick or tired. It may be that there are visitors staying at home. It could be that the usual staff members are not in class.

If there are no obvious changes, first it is important to consider if the **universal supports were in place**. We will cover universal supports in the next chapter, but they are the non-negotiables that should always be in place for all children. Sometimes these are missed or removed, but they shouldn't be.

Then, it is a process of **reviewing the situation**. There might be minor changes to the environment that you didn't notice, but the student did, such as a new smell from a seasonal tree that has just flowered outside, or a lawn mower a few houses away. **Sensory needs will also change over time**, like normal child development. They are not static. So, the supports the student require will also change over time and the student's plan needs to be reviewed regularly.

Practical example

I remember one child I worked with **became completely dysregulated overnight**. Nothing had changed at school, and he had been doing extremely well. When chatting to his parents, we discovered that they were **doing major renovations to their kitchen**. He had come home the previous day to building works, where his kitchen used to be. His mother was also stressed, understandably, because she was now feeding her family without a kitchen sink. **This change at home had a significant impact on the child at school**, and we needed to review his goals as they were not appropriate for his current circumstances.

Note from Kim

It is important to **set goals and monitor outcomes even if sensory supports have been suggested by an occupational therapist**. Sometimes supports are suggested following an assessment, but these have not been tested. The therapist will make a best guess as to what supports will help the child. But unless the child has attended further sessions or had additional reviews, **the therapist may not have tested out the supports**. The child's needs will also change over time, so if the report is older the recommendations may not be current or relevant.

Chapter 4

Creating a Sensory Plan

'Sensory strategies can be used to support optimal arousal.'

The **target** of any sensory plan should be to **support regulation and participation**. Sensory strategies can be used to both **increase and decrease arousal**. They can be used **across the day** to help a child maintain the level of arousal required to participate. They can be used **before, during or after** specific activities the child might find more challenging. There are different supports available. This chapter will explore how to get ready to use sensory strategies with different children.

Defining sensory strategies

Sensory strategies are **supports or equipment that use the senses to help organize arousal levels and engagement in activity**. Examples include wobble cushions, fidget toys, touch pressure or heavy work, a sensory diet or a sensory circuit. We will cover these in more depth in Chapter 5.

When using sensory strategies to organize a child's arousal, **the end goal should be to support participation**. The sensory strategy might help a child to focus and listen to their teacher. Or it might help them to play successfully with their friends in the playground. **We are using the senses to change and support arousal levels.** Sometimes a sensory strategy might be used to mitigate other sensations in the environment that are contributing to a child's arousal levels too.

Sensory strategy or sensory integration

Sensory strategies are informed by sensory integration theory, but they are **not the same** as Ayres® Sensory Integration treatment. Some people use these terms interchangeably, but this is incorrect.

Sensory integration

Sensory integration theory is the original theory proposed by Dr A. Jean Ayres and built on by other therapists. It explores how the brain processes sensory information to produce a response.

Sensory integration treatment is a specific approach designed by Dr Ayres. To separate it from other approaches, it is now called Ayres Sensory Integration® (ASI). This approach should **only be provided by trained therapists** who have completed additional post-graduate training. The therapy is delivered in a clinical space which includes suspended equipment (e.g., swings) and a variety of different sensory activities.

The therapy is **child led** and the therapist is supporting the child to have adaptive responses. **Adaptive responses** are successful and appropriate responses to challenging situations. The therapist will adapt the activities so that they are at the 'just right' level of challenge for the child. In each session, the therapist is looking to challenge the child's senses a little more.

Sensory strategies

Sensory strategies are **sensory activities, supports or equipment which consider Ayres' theory but do not meet the criteria for Ayres Sensory Integration**®. They are commercially readily available. No specific training is required to use sensory strategies. However, **the more informed you are the more success you will have in using them**.

Sometimes sensory strategies are **passive** and done to the child. For example, equipment like a weighted blanket assumes that deep touch pressure is calming; this assumption is drawn from Ayres' theory. But it is a passive sensory strategy which is applied to the child. It does not target multiple senses and it does not support an adaptive response.

A sensory circuit may at first look more like ASI than a weighted blanket, as it is active and sometimes child led. However, it does not target adaptive responses in the same way as ASI. Typically, circuits are quite similar through the year. They are designed to support regulation, but not necessarily to improve the processing of sensory messages in the same way as ASI.

Practical example

Noah's occupational therapy assessment indicated that his vestibular and proprioceptive systems were slower to respond to sensations. He was extremely fidgety and quite clumsy. Noah's intervention included **both sensory integration therapy and sensory strategies**. He attended weekly sessions with the occupational therapist for a term. The occupational therapist focused on his postural control and sensory responses using an ASI approach in sessions. To help at home, his mother increased his physical activity. They started going to football three times a week and he started scooting to school on his scooter. School also put in place additional movement breaks for him throughout the day. These are examples of sensory strategies.

Planning process

When choosing sensory supports, it is important that you **consider all the information you have gathered in your evaluation**. This will help you to set your goals. The strategies you choose should target the goals that you have set. It is essential to monitor the impact of the strategies and then update the child's plan.

This is the **Assess, Plan, Do, Review** cycle. The cycle is ongoing. As the child's needs or abilities change, it is important to **update their goals and strategies**. When there is a change in the task or environment, a new evaluation might be needed.

Safety and precautions

There are some **precautions** you need to be aware of before you get started. Sensory equipment, especially weighted blankets, should **not** be treated as a toy. In Chapter 5, the flag symbol (⚑) will indicate precautions which are relevant for specific equipment or activities. It is also important that you are mindful of the following information.

Over-arousal

Over-arousal occurs when a child's arousal is too high. This can lead to shut down or meltdown, concepts we explored in Chapter 2. It is important for you to be aware of the signs of over-arousal. While you need to monitor all children for this, it is extremely important to consider when working with children or adults who might be unable to communicate to you that they are uncomfortable.

Over-arousal won't just occur when you are using sensory strategies. It can occur due to an accumulation of sensory inputs during an activity. Transitions or change can also cause over-arousal for some children.

These are some signs of over-arousal:

- A change in breathing rate – usually an increase.

- A change in skin colour – typically to pale but some children or adults will also go red; this will be much less obvious on darker skin.

- A change in body/skin temperature – typically hotter.

- A change in facial expression – for example, a worried look or blank expression. The change may be subtle.

- A change in voice – monitor their pitch and tone; some children might go quiet. A very excited pitch may indicate over-arousal for some children.

- Anger, for example lashing out/biting – this is much more common in children who have limited communication skills.

They will use these behaviours to indicate discomfort in the absence of another communication strategy.

Vestibular system safety

There are two things that you must consider with the vestibular system. The first is that **too much vestibular sensory input can make some children feel like vomiting**. Remember, this is the sense that makes some people feel sick on rollercoasters. When you are using the vestibular sense, particularly with those who are sensitive, you need to be mindful of the impact it can have. A reaction might not occur straightaway, as there can sometimes be a delay.

Second, it is important to be **very respectful of a child's vestibular system tolerances**. For children who have extreme sensitivity with this sense, movement is frightening. Unstable surfaces (like wobble boards) are scary. Any activity where their feet leave the ground (e.g., swings) can be scary for them. It is important to meet them at their tolerance level. Never force them into movements they are not comfortable with. This is also one area where direct sensory integration sessions with a therapist can really help.

Neglect and trauma precautions

It is very important to be **acutely aware of children's previous experiences, especially if there is a history of neglect or trauma**. Sometimes there are sensations that trigger or replicate a negative memory from the past. It could be a specific smell or sound. This will **not necessarily make any sense to the adult observing the current situation**; however, it needs to be respected.

It is important to be **extremely careful with touch**, especially for children with a history of physical or sexual abuse. Touch input should always be **led by them**, ensuring that they're in control. It can also be helpful to seek out additional professional advice from those who are supporting the child.

Supporting sensitivity

As a rule, when there is sensitivity, **the child needs sensory supports to lower their arousal**. This means that you should reduce sensory inputs and use calming sensory activities. An important thing to remember for these children is the **impact of cumulative sensory inputs**. You need to consider sensitivity when scheduling and ensure that there is sufficient down time between activities that children might find overloading. This will help the child to lower their arousal and be more prepared for the next activity.

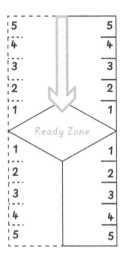

A **key sense** for helping children with sensory sensitivities is **proprioception and/or touch pressure**. Proprioceptive and touch pressure sensory inputs are thought to be very calming and very organizing to the body. They help with **downregulation**. You can provide input before, during and after activities that might be overloading for the child.

It can also help to **prepare or warn** these children in advance of sensory inputs occurring. For example, 'I'm turning the music on now.' This helps to prepare their brain for the inputs; it gives their rat brain (limbic system) a heads-up. It means that the input isn't a surprise and it helps to avoid a fight, flight, freeze response. Providing a visual schedule is another strategy that helps to prepare children for some experiences across the day.

If there are **new sensations**, letting the child have control during the first experience can often help. For example, if it's a timer, let them set it and make it beep; if it's an instrument, give it to them to play. If it's somewhere or something you can't necessarily go to in advance, stories on social media, photos or video clips showing the space or activity can be a useful way to prepare the child.

Supporting slower responses

Sensory theory suggests that individuals who are **slower to process sensory inputs** have a lower level of overall arousal. It is thought that their brains need more sensory input to understand the sensations. They **need alerting strategies to increase their arousal** so that they are ready to participate and learn.

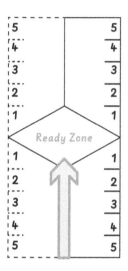

These children typically **need additional sensory input throughout the day**. It is also important to consider how higher intensity input from one sense might affect another. For example, an individual might be slower to process vestibular sensory input, but they have sensitivity to sound. So, putting them in a loud space where they can move may not regulate them as much as you had hoped.

They also need **more time to respond to sensations**. This is because their brains are slower to process them. It is important that you wait and give them this additional time. If you give them more sensory inputs before they have processed the first one, their processing time and response will be even slower.

Supporting sensory seeking

Like individuals who are slower to process sensory inputs, it is hypothesized that **sensory seekers also have a lower baseline level of arousal**. However, instead of doing nothing to help to increase this, they are actively trying to increase their arousal. This is why they are called 'seekers' and 'cravers'. They are actively seeking out more sensory inputs in order to maintain their level of alertness.

The goal for sensory seekers is to **help them regulate**. Sometimes their seeking behaviours don't support regulation, especially with movement. The additional sensory inputs don't necessarily decrease the child's arousal, it just continues to increase. They often **need structure, order and sequence to their seeking to help them regulate**. This can be done by adding structure and using a combination of alerting and organizing activities.

Note from Kim

In Chapter 2, I spoke about **sensory seeking to help regulate another sense**. Chewing is a good example. At first glance, this might appear to be a seeking behaviour, but the child might be using chewing as a sensory strategy to help to regulate noise as they are feeling overloaded. I just wanted to remind you about this again here!

Supporting dyspraxia

It is important to acknowledge that **dyspraxia impacts arousal**. Sensory strategies won't specifically change dyspraxia, but they can be used to support the impact it has on a child's arousal. Sometimes arousal will increase when a child is stuck on a task; other children could freeze or shut down. The strategies in Chapter 5 can be used to support arousal. In addition to this you can do the following:

- Give the child more time to practise and learn new skills.

- Give the child explicit instructions that include physical demonstrations.

- Help the child to break down larger tasks (don't assume they will know the steps).

- In group situations (e.g., PE), let the child watch others, rather than expecting them to go first.

- Be patient!

A final thing to remember when supporting dyspraxic children is that they **will not generalize skills well**. Generalization is the ability to **take learning from one task to another**, for example generalizing the ball skills you learned in tennis to badminton. Dyspraxic children are not always successful with this generalization. For them, badminton feels like a completely new activity they need to learn from scratch. It is important to remember to **go back to the beginning** – don't expect the learning to transfer.

Level of sensory support

There are three different levels of support you can include in your classroom and school: universal, targeted and specialist (Royal College of Occupational Therapists 2019). These increase in specificity.

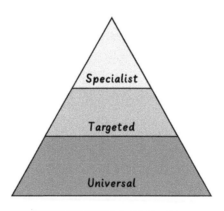

Universal supports

These are strategies or supports that are **in place for every child in the school**. They are the foundation supports that help to create a consistent and clear space for children. Universal supports are something that every team member in a school should be able to implement. They are the **non-negotiables** which are always in place.

Most schools have a behaviour policy that will outline the universal supports that are in place across the school to manage behaviour. **Sensory supports should be included in this.** If the school uses an emotional regulation programme (Chapter 6), then it should be mentioned in the policy. Having supports integrated into school policies means that all staff are on the same page and children receive consistent supports.

Examples of **universal supports** include:

- Display boards at the back of the classroom, so they are out of the child's eyeline when they face the board/teacher.

- Using the same visual resources across all classrooms (e.g., for the date or timetable).

- Staff uniform policy that recommends using unscented deodorants/no perfume.

- Whole-school sensory processing training.[1]

Targeted

Most sensory supports in this book fall into the targeted category. **Targeted supports are designed for individuals or groups.** They are not necessarily available to all children. Staff implementing them have usually received some training from a specialist teacher or from a therapist. Or they might read a book like this! In some special schools, targeted supports may be more universally available.

Examples of **targeted supports** include:

- A sensory circuit.

- Movement breaks.

- A weighted lap pad.

---

1   For example, Sensory Aware with GriffinOT – available at https://www.griffinot.com/sensory-processing-disorder-training/ Include space for QR code

Specialist

Specialist supports are typically delivered by therapists (like an occupational therapist or speech and language therapist) or highly trained staff (like the special educational needs and disabilities coordinator or therapy assistant). These supports are **very specific to an individual child**. Most readers of this book will not be delivering specialist supports.

Examples of specialist supports include:

- Ayres® Sensory Integration Therapy.

- Creation of a communication board.

Practical example

Thinking back to Noah, the sensory integration treatment sessions he attended with the occupational therapist were specialist support. The movement breaks his school started to use were targeted as they were specifically available for him. The swimming and cycling were initially targeted, but if they were embedded into his daily routine they could become a universal support.

When to use sensory supports

There is **not an exact answer to the question of when and how often**. Universal supports should always be in place. The frequency of targeted supports will vary between children. Some children need a little bit of support all the time, others can manage with supports in place for specific activities or maybe at the start and end of the day. It can be helpful to have a mix of supports that are both scheduled and flexible.

Scheduled

Scheduling of sensory supports can take various forms. **The plan should match the individual child's specific needs.** In schools, it can sometimes be tricky to schedule around these due to staffing or timetable constraints.

Examples of scheduling:

- **Time of day:** the supports are scheduled in at specific times through the day – for example, completing a sensory diet at the start of the day.

- **Transitions:** the supports are used during lesson transitions – for example, the child uses their fidget while waiting between lessons.

- **Specific environment:** the supports are used in a specific environment – for example, the child uses ear defenders in the music room and lunch hall.

- **Specific task:** the supports are used during a specific task – for example, using a weighted lap pad when seated on the carpet.

The benefits of scheduling are that the sensory supports aren't forgotten. Scheduling also helps to create routine for the child. There are also some children who need that ongoing sensory input throughout the day to stay regulated. One negative is that a child's arousal level might not always match the schedule, so it can be helpful to have some flexibility.

Flexibility

The benefit of **flexibility** is that you can **match the sensory supports to the child's arousal in the moment**. Life is not always predictable, and things will change. The schedule could say it's time for a movement break, but the child might be really focused on an activity and not need the break. There will be unexpected things that occur, for example a fire alarm or a disagreement with a peer, that impact their arousal.

Examples of flexibility:

- Providing equipment for the child **to take when they need it** – for example, ear defenders are in the room and the child can take them when they need them.

- Having **stations** in the classroom that the child can access to increase or decrease their arousal – see 'Move it Zone' and 'Chill Zone' in Chapter 5.

- **Changing the activity or schedule** to match the child's current arousal – sometimes a change will be needed in the moment.

Sensory lifestyle

To really integrate sensory supports, it can be helpful to consider how to support the child's sensory needs and responses through their entire week. **Consider where activities and supports can be included as part of their general routine every day.** The more integrated supports can be, the easier it is to complete them and the more impact they will have.

For example, if a child really benefits from additional proprioceptive input, how can this be integrated to support overall arousal? Can they attend swimming? Is it possible to cycle to and from school? Can they help in the garden? What can be included in their weekly schedule that will help them to stay well regulated?

Practical example

Using Noah as an example again, cycling to school and swimming three times a week are great examples of incorporating sensory supports into his daily life! School had scheduled movement breaks but also used them flexibly when Noah needed additional movement.

Consider co-regulation

As noted in Chapter 2, **co-regulation comes before self-regulation**. Children learn to self-regulate through co-regulation. Many children who need additional sensory supports need adult support to regulate past the age that you might expect them to. It is important for adults to **facilitate co-regulation first** before they expect students to self-regulate. You must be confident that the child has the emotional maturity and ability to self-regulate before you expect them to do this.

It may be that **the child's goals change over time to reflect this**. Initially, it may be that their goal is to access sensory strategies with adult support. Over time, this could change to accessing sensory supports independently. However, you must first make sure that the child is supported and understands how to use the sensory strategies. They should not be expected to self-regulate until they have demonstrated they are able to use strategies successfully with adult support first.

Note from Kim

One common error I see in the use of sensory supports in schools is that **children are expected to self-regulate before they can independently**. It is very important to consider the child's attachment, maturity and capacity to self-regulate. This will also change depending on the circumstances; for example, a child might be able to self-regulate when well rested but need support when they are tired.

Teacher perspective – Dr Emma Goodall

Preschool and primary school educators are used to co-regulating students, whereas with older students there is generally an expectation that they can self-regulate. This is highly problematic for students who are still developing their interoception, as without good interoception they cannot self-regulate and can be tricky to co-regulate. Positive interpersonal relationships between staff and students foster healthy attachments which also support co-regulation.

One of the most challenging things for teenagers is when they do not have the interoception awareness of their bladder. These young people cannot tell when they need to go to the bathroom until they have to go right away, which is highly problematic in a secondary school setting where students need to ask and be granted permission to leave the room. Unfortunately, by the time this permission has been asked for and granted, it may be too late for the young person.

Kids can be cruel, and toileting accidents can lead to a lifetime of bullying. Co-regulating in this context is about alerting the young person to maintain hydration while building awareness of when they might need to go to the bathroom by pointing out the observable signals to them, such as wiggling or clutching at their groin. The importance of maintaining hydration for these young people cannot be stressed enough. Without a full bladder, it is impossible to notice full bladder signals, but many of these students deliberately don't drink fluids during the school day to prevent toileting accidents!

Compassion and kindness are needed to develop trust with a teen or preteen that adults will support them and guide them so that they do not have toileting accidents, while increasing their fluid intake to enable full bladder signals to be sent and therefore potentially noticed. Being well hydrated can also increase a student's ability to focus as well as decrease the likelihood of headaches.

Other types of regulation strategies commonly used in school to support students' abilities to manage their emotions and feelings helpfully include:

- Using distraction techniques, such as asking the young person to take a box to the front office or another classroom.

- Decreasing sensory input by getting the student to go for a walk or get a drink of water from a drinking fountain out of the classroom.

- Engaging the student in a calming activity, such as those outlined in Chapter 5, to activate the part of their nervous system which biologically calms them down.

- Giving the student time to engage in sensory stims or preferred activities to lower their nervous system signals, calming them biologically.

Supporting individuals

Depending on the child, you may **need to increase or decrease their arousal level**. Some children need supports to help them be more organized, so they may need a combination of alerting and organizing activities. **The aim is to help the child to reach an optimal state of arousal where they can participate and learn.** When creating the child's plan and sensory passport, it is important to consider the following areas.

Information to consider

FACTORS THAT IMPACT AROUSAL

The factors that impact arousal, which we have already discussed, are the **first** things you need to consider before creating your plan and choosing strategies. They all need to be supported first before looking to add in sensory strategies. You must also include any specific supports that help the child, for example a visual schedule or a communication board.

CO-REGULATION OR SELF-REGULATION

The **second** thing to consider when creating a plan is the **child's ability to self-regulate**. If the child needs support to regulate, it will dictate the type of strategies you can use. An extra staff member will be needed to support co-regulation, and this needs to be considered in planning. It is helpful to include whether the child can use a strategy independently or if they need support on any documentation (e.g., sensory passport).

THE CHILD'S SENSORY RESPONSES AND GOALS

This is information you will have gathered in your **initial evaluation**. Understanding the child's sensory responses will help you to know which support strategies will be most helpful for them. This will also help you to know what universal supports can be put in place. Your plan should target the goals that you have set for the child. It is helpful to consider when the goals will be reviewed too.

Choosing sensory supports

The above information should help you to know whether you need help to increase or decrease the child's arousal. Chapter 5 outlines equipment and activities you can try, and considers changes you can make to the environment and changes you can make personally yourself.

Document your plan

It is important to **document the child's plan in a way that all adults supporting them can understand**. While longer documents may be needed for risk assessments, funding and progress records, it can be helpful to have a short one- to two-page summary which is readily accessible. This is where something like a sensory passport can be helpful.

Supporting groups

It is common for multiple children to need supports in the same class. This means you may need to **support several children at the same time**. It is important to consider each child's individual goals within the group. It is rare for all children to have the same sensory needs. This means there will need to be some personalization within the group to ensure that all children's needs are being met.

Another thing to consider is the children's impact on each other. If you have children who are sensitive to sound and children who make a lot of noise, they may not work well together. Think about which groupings of children will ensure success.

Using strategies at home

Sensory strategies can also be **used at home** to support the child. Many of the strategies in this book can be **easily transferred**. Parents can also use extra-curricular activities, like sports, to support children's sensory needs. General physical activity, like walking and cycling, can also be a helpful tool. The playground can be a great place to meet the needs of sensory seekers.

Some children may **need more down time at home**, as they find school overwhelming. Their parents might need help to identify relevant extra-curricular activities. In some cases, they may need help to put limits on the number of extra activities their children are engaging in. It may be that homework also needs to be reviewed and potentially decreased for these children.

Some parents will have found strategies that support their child to be successful at home. Listen to what they are saying. Parents are typically the experts in their children's needs, and they will be able to offer you relevant guidance. It is helpful to have open communication between home and school to share knowledge and improve understanding.

Chapter 5

Sensory Strategies

'Sensory strategies are a great tool to have in your toolbox when supporting children to regulate their arousal levels.'

Welcome to the sensory strategies chapter. I hope you have enjoyed Chapters 1–4 as I know that they will have **added to your sensory understanding**. If you haven't had a chance to read through them yet, I would highly recommend you do!

This chapter will start with **environmental considerations** and things you can consider personally when you support children with sensory needs. Next, **sensory equipment and activities** will be explored – these include lots of pictures! Finally, there will be examples of how the activities can be integrated into sensory diets, circuits and classroom supports.

The following icons will be used to indicate how the strategy will impact the child's arousal.

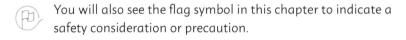
You will also see the flag symbol in this chapter to indicate a safety consideration or precaution.

Environment considerations

There are changes that can be made to the physical environment to help children participate successfully. If you are lucky enough to be building a new school, you can consider this from the initial design. Most of us are not in this position, but there are considerations we can make. There is an **environmental checklist** included in the Appendix which you can use to review your classroom.

To start, it can be helpful **just to stand in your classroom when it is empty and quiet**. What sounds do you notice? If the projector is on, there will be a slight whirr. This will be less distracting if you are further away from it. If a toilet is flushed, would it be heard? When a tap is turned on, does it squeak or do the pipes vibrate? If you're in a multistorey building, can you hear the classroom upstairs?

What can you see? How distracting are the display boards? Is there artwork hanging across the room? Are the workspaces tidy or cluttered? Are resources put away in cupboards or out on shelves? There is a huge amount of visual input every day in a classroom. The sun is another thing to consider, as it will be in different places throughout the day. Sitting directly under lighting can also be a challenge for some students.

Taste is usually not a big issue in the school environment, as it is not activated until something touches the tongue. Smell, however, is very different and can enter from anywhere. If your school has a kitchen, it is helpful to consider whether the cooking smells reach the classroom. Other children's lunches can also be considered during lunchtimes and snack times.

The environment will also encourage or inhibit movement. Some classrooms have quick access to the playground, which can be great for children who benefit from additional movement. Some schools have climbing frames and activity trails, others do not. The space available will also dictate which movement strategies you can incorporate into your day.

The environment checklist should be completed in **all rooms and areas** that the child uses. Different environments will support different children's sensory needs. For example, some children might manage in the library and classroom, but find the music room and playground overwhelming. This could be the opposite for another student. If the child is extremely successful in one space, consider what it is about this environment which is supporting them.

Practical example

I once worked with a boy who attended an autism specialist unit, which was in a multistorey building. He mentioned that there was **thunder in the building**. I was curious and asked him to let me know next time he heard it. He was hearing 'thunder' when the class above us entered and exited their room. The noise was not noticeable when only one or two children moved. But when the entire class got up to move, this boy was worrying about thunder in the building. Taking him upstairs and showing him the other classroom helped him to understand that these sounds were actually the children moving about! This significantly reduced his anxiety.

Think about yourself

You are also in the child's environment and can impact their level of arousal. Each adult also has their own sensory preferences and level of arousal, which impact the children they are working with.

Every adult in the classroom also sends out sensory messages; for example, the tone or loudness of your voice, or your own level of energy. There could be smells from your laundry liquid, or something that you ate at lunch. The table below considers common sensations.

Sense	Consider
Smell	• The scent of perfumes, deodorants, creams, styling products • The scents from laundry detergents and soaps • The scent of your breath after lunch
Vision	• The patterns on your clothing • Warning the child if you approach quickly or from behind or their side
Hearing	• Your tone and pitch of voice • The volume of your voice • If any of your clothing/accessories make sounds when you move • Warning the child before you make a noise, e.g., before you hit the drum
Touch	• If you use light or firmer touch • Letting the child know before you touch them

cont.

Sense	Consider
Proprioception	• Your reaction to the child's errors or need for additional input – is it supportive or dismissive?
Vestibular	• Your own expectations of the child, particularly if they have sensitivities • Your reaction to a child if they need movement – is it supportive or dismissive?
Interoception	• If you are regulated internally – it's not just the children, we are all processing interoceptive messages • If you are not regulated – are you the best person to provide support for the child?

Practical example

I am quite a loud and vivacious person. This can be very **over-arousing** for some children. I know that when I am working with children who have sensitivities, I need to **regulate my arousal level to be lower**. This supports them as I know that they can become quickly over-aroused by my normal level of energy. It is less effortful for me to be with children who need to increase their arousal level, as I don't have to suppress my own energy.

Sensory equipment

This chapter will give a quick overview of **sensory equipment that is available** (it is not an exhaustive list). The equipment is listed in alphabetical order. The equipment landscape is continually changing, and new products are always available. Like all sensory supports, you must monitor the effectiveness of the equipment. What is your **goal** for using it and how will you **monitor** the impact?

It can be helpful to **test equipment before investing**, especially for expensive products. Most countries have larger trade shows[1] where the companies display their products, and you can test them out. If you want

---

1   UK examples: The TES SEN Show, The Autism Show, Kidz North/South, The National Education Show.

to learn more about equipment there are additional resources on the GriffinOT website (www.griffinot.com) and in my sensory training.

Note from Kim

One comment I often hear is: '**If he/she has one then everyone in the class will want one.**' I am here to tell you today that this is **simply not true**. Children are incredibly accepting. If the adults in the classroom set the expectation that different children have different needs, then the class will quickly understand that they receive what is the best support for them. It all starts with the expectations set by the adults, and ultimately the expectations set within the whole school. **A whole-school approach** means that all teachers, support staff and students are on the same page.

Black-out tents

Dark tents are designed to reduce overall arousal. There are some very expensive ones on the market, but many schools purchase cheaper alternatives. They can be a great option for reducing arousal in children who are visually sensitive. It is a good idea to have something that can introduce light into the tent (e.g., a torch, or window) when it is needed.

Brushes

Brushing is a technique which was introduced by a therapist named Patricia Wilbarger in the 1990s. Her technique was a specific programme of regular brushing, using a surgical-style 'therapressure' brush at regular intervals through the day. The brushes provide touch pressure sensory input and the programme includes compression activities which give proprioceptive sensory input. The programme is designed to reduce touch sensitivity. To use the specific protocol, therapists have to complete training and instruct staff on how to use the programme with individual children.

These brushes are now readily available. Some children find them helpful to reduce arousal, especially if they have touch or hearing sensitivities. When using the brushes, make sure the child has given their consent, or indicated that they find the sensation calming. If the child pulls away from the brush, it is likely that they are not enjoying the sensation. I would recommend brushing in the direction of hair growth, rather than against it, which can be more alerting.

There are a lot of different brushes available these days. It can be helpful to see which one the child prefers. Some children prefer wooden/plastic massagers over the surgical brushes.

Chews

Sensory chews are designed for children who chew non-food items (e.g., their collar, pencil or shirt sleeve). Usually when a child is chewing, they are trying to lower their arousal. A sensory chew can be provided as a more appropriate and safer item for the child to chew on.

Unlike some equipment which can be shared, chews should be allocated to an individual child. They should be cleaned daily, following the manufacturer's instructions. It is also helpful to have a space or way to store them (e.g., plastic container on desk, or lanyard).

CHOOSING A CHEW

There are numerous different styles of chews. They vary in shape, texture and hardness. Before providing a chew, it is important to consider **what is increasing the child's arousal**. It is important to make changes to the environment or activity as well, to help to lower the child's arousal. A sensory chew will never be the only sensory solution required for that child.

When choosing a chew, it is helpful to consider **what and how the child chews**. If the child is chewing their sleeve, they may prefer a piece of material (e.g., a bandana) to chew on. If they are chewing at the front of their mouth, they may prefer a round chew. However, if they chew at the back of their mouth, a longer chew might be preferred so they can chew the sensory chew with their back teeth. If they are chewing on their back teeth, a tougher chew is also recommended for durability.

It is also important to consider if a sensory chew is socially and age appropriate for the child. If the child has significant learning disabilities, a sensory chew may be appropriate. However, a chew may not be appropriate for children in mainstream school who have a high level of social awareness. A pencil topper or jewellery-style chews (e.g., Chewigems) are less obvious alternatives, and, where policies allow, sugar-free chewing gum can be a great option.

Compression products

There are a variety of products that aim to **provide touch pressure for children throughout the day**. The goal of these products is to lower arousal, and so they have a calming effect. The products are usually recommended by occupational therapists and purchased by parents. Specialist schools will sometimes have Neoprene vests to use with their pupils. Here are some examples of compression products:

- Tight t-shirts (e.g., Sensational Hug T-shirt): These are inexpensive and designed to be worn under clothing. They aren't always suitable in the summer or in hotter climates. As an off-the-shelf solution, slightly smaller size t-shirts, swimming rash guards and bicycle shorts provide a similar type of touch pressure. For girls, school tights with a high amount of elasticity can provide a similar effect.

- Neoprene vests (e.g., The Bear Hug): These vests are usually made from Velcro and Neoprene. They are designed to be worn over clothing. They can be adjusted to fit the pupil's body size. They can be worn for periods during the day and are easy to put on and take off.

- Squeeze vests (e.g., Squease): These vests can be inflated and deflated with air as required. They are like a scuba-diving buoyancy control device. When inflated, the vest gives the child's body a big squeeze. They are expensive, and it's highly recommended they are tested first.

- Compression garments: These are like compression garments for burns. They are expensive and typically are only provided following specialist assessment and private funding.

Dynamic seating

There are **numerous styles** of dynamic chairs available. They include chairs like the Zuma rocker, Hokki and Activ Stools and ball chairs. The aim of all sensory chairs is to help children with attention issues to focus. They are designed to increase arousal. Wobble cushions fit in here too, but they will be discussed in more detail below.

The chairs are designed to provide children with movement that is **less distracting and safer** than the movements they may be doing to help keep themselves alert and focused. The purpose of the dynamic seating is to allow these children to move about in a more appropriate way. So, rather than rocking on their chair or moving about the classroom, the dynamic seating gives the child a way to move about in their seat.

When choosing dynamic seating, it is helpful to test the equipment with the child before purchasing it. Some companies will do short trials, and most of them exhibit at the trade shows mentioned earlier. Some schools may have one which they can test with children before they purchase more. Also, make sure you consider whether the seating will be the right size to match your existing school furniture (e.g., do the arms fit under the tables in your classroom?) and that you have sufficient storage space.

Ear defenders

Ear defenders are designed to **block out additional sounds in the environment**. They are readily available and inexpensive. They are a fantastic piece of equipment to support children who experience sensitivity to sounds. Typically, they are used during noisier periods, but some children choose to wear them most of the time. It is important that children learn to use them independently.

Ear defenders won't work for all pupils, as some pupils don't like wearing them because they muffle sounds. Some children prefer ear plugs. Others prefer noise-cancelling headphones, which can be used without music playing. This is because noise-cancelling headphones remove and don't muffle sounds in the same way as ear defenders do. If a child has a particularly large head, adult gardening ear protectors come in larger sizes.

Fidget toys

These can be a useful solution for pupils who are **constantly fiddling at their desk**. The goal of a fidget toy is to give the pupil a more appropriate and less distracting item to fiddle with. It is important to choose a toy which is silent and will not distract other pupils in the classroom. It's useful to find one that is robust as well. Some examples of everyday objects you could use include:

- Blu Tack

- A small piece of fabric

- A keyring

- A Lego piece or person

- A rubber snake toy

- A stress ball.

Commercially available products include:

- Tangles
- Stretchy men
- Koosh balls
- Twist and lock blocks

- Theraputty.

Lycra

Lycra, or a stretch knit fabric, is a great way to provide **touch pressure and proprioceptive sensory input**. This typically helps with lowering arousal. Lycra body bags and tunnels are commercially available. Some people also sew their own. It is important that the child can easily remove themselves from the bag or tunnel.

Practical example

One child I worked with used a Lycra body bag to decrease his arousal and help him stay seated during assembly. The touch pressure from the Lycra lowered his arousal. It also gave him additional feedback about where his body was, so he didn't need to fidget about.

Scooter board

Scooter boards are a great way to provide **proprioceptive and vestibular sensory inputs**. There are some examples of how to use them in the **activities section**. When using a scooter board, it is important that you follow these **safety rules**:

- An adult must always supervise.
- There must be sufficient space to use the board.
- The individual can sit or lie on the board.

- When on their stomach, encourage the child to pull forward using their hands, and keep their legs lifted.

- Some children may need to be taught to keep their hands away from the wheels.

- When lying on the back or sitting it is easier to push backwards with the feet.

- The child must NEVER stand on the scooter board; these are NOT like skateboards and they will slide out and cause injury.

- Ensure that there is no loose/long clothing that can get caught under the wheels (e.g., sweaters, scarfs, ties, long hair).

Sensory rooms (Snoezelen rooms)

These are rooms with **lights, bubble tubes, music and sometimes vibrating surfaces**. The goal of these rooms is to create a relaxing space that helps to reduce agitation and anxiety. The space can also be used to engage the child, stimulate reactions and encourage communication.

These rooms can be used in a variety of ways. Each room will have different equipment. If you are not sure how to use the equipment, check with your therapist or the company that installed the room. **It is essential that you have a goal for using the room as this will dictate how you use it.**

Goals could include:

- regulation and calming

- interaction, joint attention and turn taking

- choosing, including symbol use

- learning how to use switches.

If the goal is regulation, then it is important to **find the equipment that helps the child to regulate**. This will be different for every child, and you will need to decide which equipment or equipment combination works best for which child. It is common for these rooms to be used inefficiently and for children to be less regulated after being in them. This is why it's important to have a plan for each individual child.

Learn more

The book *Multiple Multi-Sensory Rooms: Myth Busting the Magic* by Joanna Grace (2019, Routledge) explores tips and strategies for using these rooms.

Vibration

Vibration can be a useful sensory input for some children. It is carried through the touch sense and **can both increase and decrease arousal**. There are a variety of products available. When searching, **it is best to use specific sensory product sites**, as a general search for 'vibrating toys' will not return what you are looking for. Here are some products that are available:

- Cushions for both sitting on and putting feet on
- Longer snake-like tubes
- Toys for the mouth like the Z-vibe
- Hand-held massagers (also commercially available)
- Vibrating gym plates.

When using vibrations, **the child must have control over what is being done**. If you're putting the items on the child, make sure you look for indicators that they want more. Always make sure they can ask you to stop, either verbally or non-verbally. Some children don't like the noise which the vibration makes. You can sometimes get around this if you let them be in control of the on/off switch, so they learn that the noise is coming from the item.

Start with the child's hands and arms, then move to their back and legs. Some children will really like the feeling of vibration on their face, but it is important to **avoid** this for children with epilepsy as it may cause a seizure. Also ensure that the vibration is **not used** near the child's genitals. If the child is using the item themselves, be mindful of where the cushion or items are positioned.

Visual displays

Slow moving visual displays can be very calming. Bubble tubes are a classic example, but they come in many forms. Fish tanks or videos of fish tanks are another example. There are liquid timers and ooze tubes. Some children love snow globes. You can make your own glitter tube using a sealed container, glitter and water. There are also apps available which have different visual effects when you touch the screen (e.g., Fluidity). Some children also love the visualizations some music players (e.g., Windows Media Player, iTunes) show when music is playing.

Weighted products

These products come in different shapes and sizes. They provide touch pressure, and if the child is moving under them or carrying them, they also provide additional proprioceptive sensory input. The goal of weighted products is to lower arousal, or to calm.

SAFETY

These products are not toys. Unfortunately, there is a well-documented case in Canada where a child died after being rolled up in a weighted blanket and left unsupervised. The blanket restricted their breathing and they passed away. The weighted products should weigh no more than 10 per cent of the child's body weight. It is essential that the child is **always monitored** when using weighted products, especially weighted blankets.

WEIGHTED BLANKETS

Weighted blankets are large and usually available in single and double-bed sizes. They can be used over the top of the child in a variety of positions.

It's important these are monitored closely. Make sure **you can always see the child's face and you can monitor their breathing**. Only allow the child to put their face under the blanket if they are independently able to move out from under it and when they can verbally respond to you that they are okay.

NEVER leave the pupil alone under the blanket. While weighted blankets can be helpful, there are some risks associated with using them. Make sure there is a clear safety policy in place at school and all staff are aware of the risks.

WEIGHTED LAP/SHOULDER PADS

Weighted lap pads and animals are designed to sit on the child's lap. They can be great for children who have poor proprioceptive awareness, as they give the child extra feedback about where they are. They can decrease their fidgeting and help them to stay in their space, especially on the floor. They can also be used with young children, instead of a blanket.

Weighted shoulder pads are designed to sit on the child's shoulders. Some children don't like the feel of the pad on their neck, and it can be difficult to find shoulder pads that fit well. The snake-shaped animals are sometimes a better option, as they can be draped around the neck and shoulders. Larger lap pads can also be folded in half long ways and draped over the shoulders for the same effect.

WEIGHTED VESTS
Weighted vests are designed to be worn over the top of clothing. They are usually more successful than shoulder pads, as they don't fall off. When purchasing these for school, it is helpful to have vests with removable weights so you can adjust the weight to suit the child.

Wobble cushions

Wobble cushions are air-filled plastic cushions which provide an unstable surface for children to sit on. They are typically disc or wedge shaped and are designed to **allow children to move about while seated in their chair**. The goal of weighted cushions is to increase arousal. They are primarily designed for movement seekers but can sometimes help children who are slower to respond to movement. Children who may benefit include those who:

- rock in their chair

- frequently move about in their seat or constantly approach the teacher

- slump over, and struggle to focus.

Wobble cushions are an inexpensive piece of equipment, but they are not a one-size-fits-all solution. Some children dislike the feeling of the cushion, others tire quickly because of the extra effort it takes to sit on the cushion. For some children, they don't make any difference.

In order to be effective, they must be **inflated correctly**.[2] When the child sits on the cushion, the base should remain flat, but there will be

---

2   If you're unsure, watch this video: www.griffinot.com/ ten-tips-wobble-cushions-classroom

some movement in the cushion itself. This will allow the child to move in a more appropriate way than rocking on their chair. If there is too much air, the base will be very unstable, and if there is too little, the cushion won't provide any movement. The child's feet must touch the floor when they are sitting on the cushion, otherwise they will be unstable.

Calming and organizing activities

The activities in this section **typically help with decreasing arousal**. You can use them as one-off activities, or as part of a sensory diet or sensory circuit. They can also be included in your calm zones and 'Move it Zones'. It is recommended that adults supervise all activities initially, until they are confident children can complete them safely and independently.

Yoga

Space
Varies depending on pose

Sense/s targeting
Proprioception, vestibular,

Equipment
Videos can help
Mat (optional)

Arousal goal
Decrease

Tips

- Stretching poses provide more proprioceptive sensory input

- Poses where the head is down give more vestibular sensory input

- Consider a morning or lunchtime yoga club

Activities

WARRIOR

- Child positions their feet out wide

- Their right foot turns out to the right, the left foot stays facing straight

- They stretch their arms out at shoulder level

- They bend to the right until the right knee is over the right ankle

- Hold for 5–20 seconds and swap sides

CHAIR

- Child positions their feet hip-width apart

- Their hips go backwards, as if they are sitting down in a chair

- Their arms stretch up and out, straight in front

- Hold for 5–20 seconds and repeat

TRIANGLE

- Child positions their feet out wide

- Their arms stretch out to shoulder level

- Keeping arms straight, they bend over to the right until the right hand touches the right leg

- Hold for 5–20 seconds and swap sides

TREE

- Child positions their feet hip-width apart

- They rotate their right knee out and place their right foot onto their right ankle

- They lift their hands up and stretch up tall

- Hold for 5–20 seconds and swap sides

- As balance improves, their foot can be placed further up on their leg

EAGLE ARMS

- Child stretches arms out to the side

- While stretched, they bring them to the centre with their right arm underneath their left

- They bend their elbows so that their fingertips face the ceiling

- They cross hands over so that their palms touch

- They keep their arms at shoulder level but stretch to the ceiling with each in-breath

- Hold for 5–20 seconds and swap sides

FROG

- Child positions their feet out wide

- They keep their back straight

- They crouch down until their hands touch the floor

- Hold for 5–30 seconds

CAT/COW

- Child starts on all fours

- On their in-breath, they drop their head and hips so their back curls up like a cat stretch

- On their out-breath, they swap their head and hip positions so their back drops down

- Repeat slowly with breath 10–20 times

COBRA

- Child lies on the floor with their body out straight

- They position their hands beside their shoulders

- They lift their head and chest up to stretch

- This position can be held for 5–20 seconds

- Alternatively, it can be sequenced with the breath, stretching on the in-breath, relaxing on the out-breath

DOWNWARD DOG

- Child starts on all fours, with their hands slightly wider than their shoulders

- They lift their hips up

- Their hands and feet stay in the same position

- Their head faces down, but their spine remains in line

- Hold for 5–20 seconds

CHILD'S POSE

- Child starts on all fours, positioning their hands slightly wider than their shoulders

- They move their knees out so that their toes touch together

- As they move their hips back to sit on their feet, their head will go down

- They must keep their hands stretching forward

- Hold for 10–60 seconds

Additional resources

- Jamie at Cosmic Kids: https://cosmickids.com (also on YouTube)

- Yoga Pretzels Cards

- Twinkl Yoga Cards

Meditation and breathing

Space
Seated

Sense/s targeting
Interoception, proprioception

Equipment
Videos can help

Arousal goal

Decrease

Tips

- Match the length of the meditation to the child's ability

- This is a great way to start the day and to reorganize after lunch

Activities

FINGER BREATHING

- Child stretches open the fingers of one hand

- They use the index finger of their other hand to slowly trace up and down the fingers

- They breathe in as their finger traces up, and out as it traces down

- Repeat 3–5 times

SQUARE BREATHING

- Child imagines a square and breathes in the following sequences:

  - Breath in for a count of 4–5

  - Hold for a count of 4–5

  - Breath out for a count of 4–5

  - Hold for a count of 4–5

- Videos (1, 3, 5 minutes) available on the GriffinOT YouTube channel

TRIANGLE BREATHING

- Child imagines a triangle and breathes in the followings sequence:

  - Breathe in for a count of 3–4

  - Hold for a count of 3–4

  - Breathe out for a count of 6–8

- Videos (1, 3, 5 minutes) available on the GriffinOT YouTube channel

ELEPHANT BREATH

- Child stretches their arms up tall on the in-breath

- They then drop them down between their legs on the out-breath

- They breathe slowly for a maximum of 15 breaths

- Monitor the child to ensure they do not become dizzy

Additional resources

- Breathing videos at GriffinOT: www.youtube.com/c/GriffinOT

- Jamie at Cosmic Kids: https://cosmickids.com (also on YouTube)

- GoNoodle relaxation/breathing videos: www.gonoodle.com

- Moovlee have some breathing meditations on YouTube: www.youtube.com/c/Moovlee

- Smiling Mind has free children's meditations: www.smilingmind.com.au

- Headspace subscription (paid version) has children's content: www.headspace.com

Yoga ball or roll activities – calming/organizing

Space
Large clear space

Sense/s targeting
Proprioception, vestibular

Equipment
45–75cm yoga (therapy) ball

Arousal goal
Decrease/Organize

Tips

- Standard size is 65cm; 45, 55 and 75cm are also available

- Use a smaller ball for shorter children and a bigger one for taller teenagers

- A peanut/cylinder roll is much more stable, and helpful for children with very poor postural control or those with vestibular sensitivity

- Movement must always be slow; faster movements will increase arousal

- Adult supervision is always required

- Ensure there is adequate clear space for the activity; use mats if the child is too unstable

Activities

HEAD OVER BALL

- Child kneels with the ball in front of them

- They place their tummy over the ball, so their head hangs down and their hands touch the ground

- The ball must be small enough for the child's hands and knees to be on the floor still when in this position

- Child can stay still, or rock slowly forwards and backwards, or gently side to side

- Closing the eyes can also lower arousal

BALL WALKOUTS

- Child kneels with the ball in front of them

- They put their tummy over the ball and touch the ground with their hands

- They walk slowly forwards with their hands until their knees are touching the ball

- They can hold here for 5 seconds

- They walk their hands back slowly and repeat the movement

- Ensure the child isn't pushing forwards quickly

BALL HIT

- This activity requires a clear space or hallway

- Child lies on their stomach

- Adult stands back from the child

- Child lifts their hands up, so their palms are facing the adult

- Adult throws the ball towards the child's hands and they hit it back

- This activity can be quite tiring, so repeat and rest as needed

BALL: BELLY BALL

- This activity needs to be done in pairs

- Some children need to be paired with an adult initially

- It's a great activity for children to do in groups

- Children need to work in pairs to move the ball across the room

- Sideways is usually easier than backwards/forwards

- Set up a course for the children to navigate through

Additional resources

- I explore postural control and use of therapy balls in further depth in Level 3 of my sensory training: www.griffinot.com/sensory-processing-disorder-training

Resistance band

Space
Standing arm's width

Sense/s targeting
Proprioception

Equipment
Resistance band (e.g., Theraband®)

Arousal goal
Decrease/Organize

Tips

- Ensure that the children move slowly and with control

- Avoid releasing the band quickly

- Bands come in different strengths; there should be some tension when the child pulls the band, but they shouldn't be straining. Medium strength is a good place to start, but light and heavy might be needed for students who find medium too hard or too easy to pull

- Different brands use different colours for their band strengths, so always check the description, rather than relying on colour when you're purchasing

- If you purchase a roll, cut 70–100cm lengths

   •   Adult supervision is recommended until the child demonstrates they are safe

Activities

THERABAND: ARM STRETCH

- Make sure the child holds the band in a position that gives some tension when it is stretched (this will depend on the band length)

- Child brings hands together

- Then they stretch out as wide as they can

- They keep their arms at shoulder level

- Hold for 2–10 seconds

- Repeat

- If the child can't manage to hold a longer piece of band in the middle, they will need a shorter piece

BEHIND SHOULDERS

- Child positions the band behind their shoulders at scapular height

- Never let the band sit on their neck – it MUST be on their scapulars

- Pull the band forward, either with one or two hands; hold for 2–10 seconds

- Repeat

STAND AND PULL

- Child stands in the middle of the band

- They hold it with either hand and stretch the band up

- Hold for 2–10 seconds

- Repeat

Heavy work

Space
Depends on activity

Sense/s targeting
Proprioception

Optional equipment
Some children find marks on the wall to press (e.g., hand prints) helpful
Slam ball
Heavy item to carry (e.g., backpack with water bottle and book in it/box of books/thick book)

Arousal goal
Decrease/Organize

Tips

- Heavy work includes anything that gives resistance to the proprioceptors

- The resistance band and ball activities in this section are also heavy work type activities

- If you're using a slam ball or heavy item, match this to the child's size

Activities

HAND PRESS

- Child puts their palms together at their chest
- They press them together and hold for 5–10 seconds
- Repeat 5–10 times

FINGER PULL

- Child interlocks their fingers together at their chest
- They try to pull them apart for 5–10 seconds
- Repeat 5–10 times

CHAIR PRESS-UP

- Ensure the child is on firm and stable seating
- Child places their palms firmly on the edge of the chair
- They lift themselves up off the chair using their arms
- Hold for 2–10 seconds
- Repeat

WALL PRESS

- Child stands arm's distance from and facing the wall
- They keep their feet still and place their palms firmly on the wall
- They bend their arms to a press-up position on the wall and push back
- Repeat

PRESS-UPS/PLANK

- Child places their hands and feet on the ground in a plank press-up position
- They hold this position (plank)
- Or, do press-ups

SLAM BAG

- Activity requires a gym slam bag/ball
- Adult supervision is always recommended
- Ensure that the child can lift the ball up without difficulty – they shouldn't be straining their back, and if they are it's too heavy
- Child lifts the slam bag up above their head (by bending their knees and keeping their back straight ⓟ)
- Child throws the slam bag down to the floor (they must be taught to throw downwards, not forwards ⓟ)
- Repeat

CRAB KICKS

- Child sits and puts their hands behind them
- They lift their bottom up into the air by pushing through their hands and feet
- They kick one foot up and put it down
- Then they kick the other foot up and put it down

CRUNCH

- Child lies on their back with their feet flat on the ground

- They curl up into a sit-up curl

- Hold for 5–10 seconds and repeat

- Make sure they keep their chin curled

WALL WALK

- Not all children can do this as they need to have reasonable postural control

- Reasonable space and a clear wall are needed for this position

- The child positions themselves on all fours with their feet facing the wall

- They walk their feet up the wall so they are in a handstand position

- They can hold for 5–10 seconds and then walk down

Additional resources

- GriffinOT has a slow movement playlist on their YouTube channel: www.youtube.com/c/GriffinOT

Linear swinging

Space
Sufficient for swing

Sense/s targeting
Vestibular

Equipment
Swing

Arousal goal
Decrease

Tips

- Linear refers to moving forwards and backwards

- The motion should be rhythmical and slow

Activities

- Swinging for a specific amount of time on a swing

- Use the swing as part of a sensory diet or circuit

Additional resources

- Linear movement can also be achieved using the head over the ball yoga ball

- A rocking chair provides similar input

- Consider your playground equipment too

Touch pressure

Space
Seated

Sense/s targeting
Touch pressure

Equipment
Brushes (optional)

Arousal goal
Decrease

Tips

- A '**caring c**' hand position must always be used. Keep your fingers together and apply pressure with the palm, NOT the fingers. **NEVER curl the fingers** around the child's limbs. Keep your fingertips straight so they create a wide c shape. This is essential to avoid bruising the child

- **The child must give permission** for you to touch them and have control of when you stop

- Touch pressure should **NEVER** be used to restrain a child

Activities
SHOULDER SQUEEZE

- Keep your palm straight or use a 'caring c'
- Ask the child permission to touch their arms
- Put one hand on each upper arm
- Apply firm pressure, so that you're squeezing your hands together to the centre, rather than squeezing your hands around the child's arms
- Hold for 10–30 seconds and repeat if the child wishes
- This activity is usually easier to complete from behind the child. You must be able to monitor their responses to understand when they would like more or to stop. A mirror or another adult can be helpful to see a child's facial expressions

TOUCH PRESSURE WITH BRUSH

- Surgical-style brushes can also be used to apply touch pressure
- Ensure that you have the child's permission to brush the skin
- Only brush the arms, hands or legs (avoid the feet)
- Use one hand under the limb to hold it steady
- Using some pressure, brush in a downward motion, against the direction of hair growth
- Lift and repeat
- This can be continued until the child is calm or requests you to stop
- Some children will use the brush independently at their desk, or in the calm space

Oral activities – calming

Space
Depends on activity

Sense/s targeting
Proprioception, interoception

Equipment
See activities below

Arousal goal
Decrease/Organize

Tips

- Blowing bubbles is a great way to help to regulate breathing for children who find it difficult to control their breathing

- A cleaning schedule must be in place for any oral toys that are shared between children

- Chewy foods are also very organizing (e.g., dried fruit, chewing gum)

Activities
BUBBLES

- This activity is exactly what it says on the tin

- Bubble blower pipes/straws are available for children who don't have the lip-closure skills for regular bubble blowing

BUBBLE MOUNTAIN

- This works well in the sink or outside, as it can become messy!

- Children need to know the difference between suck and blow – but they usually learn quite quickly not to suck!

- Put detergent into a bowl and fill two-thirds of the bowl with water

- The child puts their straw into the water and blows so that they make bubbles on top of the water

- Use thicker straws (or clean garden hose pipe) to make the activity even harder

STRAW RACES

- Child uses the straw to blow the Styrofoam along

- Initially, just blowing it off a table can be fun

- If they can stay regulated, children can have races to see how quickly they can move the foam from one end to the other using just their breath

STRAW MAZE

- Mark out a maze on the table or ground (use chalk/markers or tape)

- Child uses the straw to blow the Styrofoam along the path

- Add in curved lines to make it even harder

- Make tunnels with blocks or cardboard tubes

Additional resources

- Whistles and other wind instruments can also be used. These need to be matched to children's sound tolerance levels

- Party blowers can also be fun (but again are quite noisy)

Warm temperature

Space
Small

Sense/s targeting
Touch, interoception

Equipment
See below in activities

Arousal goal
Decrease

Tips

- Ensure that the item is not too hot that it will burn the child!

- Integrate the warm object into a routine (e.g., after lunch, during quiet reading)

Activities

- Warm drink – this could just be warm water but could also include flavours like lemon, ginger or mint

- Heat pack – a variety of commercial ones are available; some have a lavender scent which can be calming for some

- Consider the room temperature, especially during winter in cold countries!

Scooter board – calming/organizing

Space
Large space to move on board

Sense/s targeting
Proprioception, vestibular, interoception

Equipment
Scooter board
Markers or cones (optional)
Rope (optional; skipping rope will work)

Arousal goal
Decrease/Organize

Tips

- The child must always be supervised; please see scooter board rules in the equipment section too

- Ensure that the child's clothing is suitable and hair is tied up

- Using the board on carpet will increase the resistance

Activities
SCOOTER PULL

- Child lies on their stomach on the board

- They use their hands to move the board along the floor

- Use markers or floor markings to create a course to follow

- Use markers to create a slalom

- *Avoid* spinning or fast movement as this can be alerting

SCOOTER ROPE PULL

- Ensure adult has *no* shoulder, back, hip or knee pain, or other injuries which may be exacerbated by doing this activity

- Child lies on their stomach on the board

- Put the rope in front of the child and stretch it out

- The child needs to pull themselves along the rope until they reach the adult

- The adult can also put the rope in a position for the child to move over to using their hands

Alerting activities

Scooter board – alerting

Space
Large space to move on board

Sense/s targeting
Vestibular, proprioception

Equipment
Scooter board
Markers or cones (optional)

Arousal goal

Increase

Tips

- The child must always be supervised. See scooter board rules in the equipment section too

- Ensure that the child's clothing is suitable and hair is tied up

- Using the board on wooden floors will decrease the resistance and increase the speed

Activities

SCOOTER TUMMY MOVE

- Child lies on their stomach on the board

- They use their hands to move the board along the floor

- Use speed to increase the vestibular input

- Use markers or floor markings to create a course to follow

- Use markers to create a slalom

SCOOTER SPIN

- Child lies on their stomach on the board

- They use their hands to move the board around in a circle, pivoting on their stomach

- Complete a maximum of ten rotations in each direction

- Ensure that the child does not become too over-aroused; use direction changes and straight movement between spins

SCOOTER PUSH

- This activity only works in a large space where there is a stable wall which the child can push off

- Child lies on their stomach on the board

- They move backwards to the wall, crouching their toes to the wall

- They push off the wall and go forward quickly

- Ensure that the child keeps their hands up off the floor when they are moving (this can take practice!)

- Measure how far the child gets each time

SCOOTER BACK MOVE

- Child lies on their back

- Ensure that their head is either on the board or tucked up so that it is not touching the floor

- They push the board with their feet

- Use markers or floor markings to create a course to follow

Yoga ball or roll activities – alerting

Space
Large, clear space

Sense/s targeting
Vestibular

Equipment
45–75cm yoga (therapy) ball

Arousal goal
Increase

Tips

- Standard size is 65cm, but 45, 55 and 75cm are also available

- Use a smaller ball for shorter children and a bigger one for taller teenagers

- A peanut/cylinder roll is much more stable, and helpful for children with very poor postural control or those with vestibular sensitivity

- Movement must always be **controlled** so that the child does not injure themselves

- Adult supervision is always required

- Ensure that there is adequate clear space for the activity, and use mats if the child is too unstable

Activities

BALL BOUNCING

- Child sits on the ball
- Ensure that the child keeps their feet on the ground
- Child bounces their body up and down
- Add counting and go/stop if structure is required
- If the child has the postural stability, they can also bounce around the ball and change directions each time they come back to the centre

BALL TWIST

- Child sits on the ball
- Ensure that the child keeps their feet on the ground
- Child twists to the right to touch their back, then they twist to the left
- Repeat a maximum of ten times
- If the adult stands behind the child, they can high five each other as the child turns

BALL UP AND DOWN

- Child holds the ball between both hands

- They stretch up tall

- Then bend over

- Repeat 10–20 times

Additional resources

- Sensory Aware with GriffinOT explores postural control and use of therapy balls in further depth: www.griffinot.com/ sensory-processing-disorder-training

Cold temperature

Space
Small

Sense/s targeting
Touch, interoception

Equipment
See below in activities

Arousal goal
Increase

Tips

- Ensure that the item is not too cold; where relevant, use a cover to ensure that it does not create an ice burn

Activities

- Cold compress or ice pack on neck
- Cooler space in room/cooler room temperature
- Cold drink

Movement

Space
Depends on activity

Sense/s targeting
Vestibular, proprioception

Equipment
See activities below

Arousal goal
Increase

Tips

- Some children may need structure added (see next chapter) to ensure that they organize, rather than become over-aroused
- Activities will depend on the space, equipment and resources you have at your own school

Activities

JUMPING

- Jumping is a great way to increase arousal

- This can be done on the spot next to the child's desk

- The child can also jump left to right over an imaginary line

- They can jump forwards and backwards

- If there is space, they can jump around the space

- Changing direction or counting adds structure

STAR JUMPS (JUMPING JACKS)

- As expected, the child jumps feet out with coordinating hands, making a star shape

- Make it harder by keeping the feet up in their air between jumps

- The child can also explode up from a crouched position into their star

RUNNING

- Child runs on the spot

- They can count the number of steps if needed, or use a timer for a number of minutes

- Put a spot on the ground if the child needs a physical marker

ANKLE TAPS

- Child opens their right leg out to the side

- Then they swing it back in

- They tap their left ankle as it swings out to the side

- They keep swapping sides like a pendulum

TWIST

- Child stretches their arms out to the side and then twists their body right to left

- Their arms will wrap around to the back and then unravel

- Ensure that the child doesn't become dizzy

- This activity can also be completed at the child's desk

DOWN AND UP

- Child stretches up tall

- Then they drop their head down to their feet

- Repeat but ensure that the child does not become dizzy

- This activity can also be

completed at the child's desk, and they can stand up when stretching up

WINDMILL

- Child starts with their arms stretched out

- Then they touch their right hand to their left leg

- They stand up and swap sides

Additional resources

- Running and ball games can also be used

- Larger equipment can also be used if it is available (e.g., trampolines, swings, bikes, scooters, slides, playground equipment)

- GoNoodle has fantastic dancing resources: www.gonoodle.com

- GriffinOT has a Brain Break playlist on its YouTube channel: www.youtube.com/c/GriffinOT

Oral activities – alerting

Space
Small

Sense/s targeting
Proprioception, touch

Equipment
See activities below

Arousal goal
Increase

Tips

- Ensure that the child has no allergies to suggested items

Activities

- Crunching ice
- Crunchy food (e.g., raw carrots, rice/corn cakes)

Adding structure
Some children who seek out additional movement are not organized by this sensory input. The sensations continue to increase their arousal. These children require structure to help organize their brains. This can be done in a variety of ways:

- Counting: The child needs to count while doing the movement and stop at a pre-determined number.

- Freeze/Go: The child needs to freeze when the adult requests. This can also be done with music.

- Movement course: The child needs to complete the movements in a set order.

- Memory: The child is given a plan they need to follow at the start – for example, scoot to the red cone, then the blue one, then the green one.

- Matching: The child needs to match items while moving – for example, take all of the red beanbags to the red box; sort the numbers and letters into different sides of the room; find the letters to make different words.

- Dance routines.

The other way to support organization for these children is to include both alerting and calming activities in the child's routine. So, they might do five minutes of structured movement, followed by two heavy work activities. It can sometimes help to use a ratio of one alerting activity to one calming, but it depends on the child.

Sensory diets

Sensory diets are a list of sensory activities that the child completes at certain points throughout the day to help with their regulation. The sensory activities might include movement, a calm break or yoga. Often, they are used for fidgety children and those who struggle to pay attention, but they can also help children who are easily overloaded. They are commonly suggested as a support for individuals with sensory processing differences, including those with autism.

The reason the term 'diet' is used is because early authors suggested that our bodies need sensations in the same way they need food. This analogy was used to describe how sensations can help to both increase and decrease arousal. A traditional sensory diet will include a timetabled list of sensory activities to be used throughout the day to support arousal.

Occupational therapists will typically complete a sensory profile and assessment to determine the best supports for an individual's sensory diet. They will work with the child, their family and their teachers to determine the best supports to put in place. This will vary depending on the individual's needs and the environment and equipment that are available. There is no one-size-fits-all and every child's needs are different.

Every activity suggested in this section can be used in a sensory diet. It is helpful to have activities that can be used in the moment, as days are never going to be completely predictable. Some flexibility is also recommended: if the child is really engaged in an activity, they may not need their movement break in that exact moment.

Finally, it can be helpful to link regulation strategies to the daily routine. This stops them from being forgotten! It also helps to create predictability and independence for the child.

There are examples of sensory diets in the case studies at the end of the book.

Sensory circuits

A sensory circuit is **a group of sensory activities used to support an individual's arousal**. The sensory circuit should include sensory activities that help the individual to regulate. It might include movement activities which help the student to become more alert, or it could include proprio-ceptive-based activities to help a child get organized. It may include a mix of the two.

Usually, **the circuit is set up in a structured order**. So, there is a group of sensory activities for the children to work through. They might do the circuit once or it might be something they repeat multiple times. The space and equipment available will also dictate what the circuit will look like.

The biggest challenge with using sensory circuits in schools is **making sure that they meet the individual needs of each child**. This means that you may need to direct different children to different parts of the circuit, or have them complete the circuit in a different order.

Note from Kim

There have been times where I have observed the morning 'sensory circuit' with a feeling of dread in my stomach. Movement activities have been set up as a one-size-fits-all solution. There is no structure. The children are making up their own thing. **It is unclear what the goals are.** I cannot say that the circuit supports regulation for many of the children. If you are using sensory circuits, make sure you have individual goals in mind. If it helps, **pretend I'm in the room observing with a smile on my face because I can see exactly how you are supporting the children's regulation**.

Move it Zone

A 'Move it Zone' is a great way to create independence with movement breaks. It is **a small space, either in the classroom or in the corridor, which includes movement activities**. These can be set up as a display, in a box, or on a key ring. It is recommended that four or five activities are included. These can be changed each week or fortnight for variety.

Children can **access the space when they need to increase their arousal and alertness**. Initially, they might need adult support to identify when to go to the space and how to do the activities appropriately. Over time, they should be able to access it independently. Allow all children in the class to access the space for full inclusion.

Calm zone

A calm zone is **a quiet space the child can go to downregulate**. It can include breathing activities, resistance movements, and other equipment the child finds calming. There might be a book or colouring-in sheets if this helps the child. The child might need help to access this space initially, but over time they can learn to use it independently.

The key thing about the calm zone is that it needs to be calm! It must be quiet and free of distractions. It should contain items that will help the child to regulate. Children should be encouraged to use it as a regulation space and understand it is not a space where they are 'in trouble'.

Everyday activities

There are many opportunities for regulation using everyday activities. Every time we move, we activate the senses.

- The Daily Mile – walking one mile at the start of the school day (https://thedailymile.co.uk).

- Playground equipment – this varies from school to school and park to park, but many playgrounds have items you can climb and balance on.

- Forest school has multiple opportunities for sensory regulation. Digging, carrying, pushing and pulling activate the proprioceptors. Balancing, crawling and running activate the vestibular system. Being outside in nature can also have a calming effect.

- Snacks and lunch – consider what foods will provide more proprioceptive input when the child is eating, for example dried fruit.

- Lunch and break time – consider what the child needs. Some children benefit from quiet indoor activities (e.g., Lego, games or reading club). Other children benefit from the movement running about in the playground provides. Match the lunchtime activities to the child's needs.

- After-school activities – swimming, cycling, rock climbing, ballet, gymnastics and martial arts provide significant amounts of proprioceptive and vestibular sensory input.

- Gardening and laundry are great heavy work activities.

- Classroom helper is a great role for children who need more movement. Can they do all of the trips to the office during the day?

Other strategies

While sensory strategies can have a powerful impact, it's good to remember there are many other activities that can help children to regulate. These are readily available in the classroom and at home.

- Having a drink

- Having a snack (e.g., rice cake)

- Reading

- Colouring in

- Doing puzzles

- Sorting (coloured maths counters are great for this!)

- Listening to favourite song/piece of music

- Going for a short walk.

When the child 'won't engage'

To finish this chapter, we will consider the situation where the child **won't engage** in the sensory activities you have planned. Sometimes this can occur because the child **doesn't have the coordination skills to participate**. In this case, it's important to use activities that the child is successful with. When a child needs to regulate, this is not a time to be teaching them new skills, or to be stretching their ability. The activities need to be easily accessible.

The other time this commonly occurs is **when a child does not feel safe in a regulated state**. Unfortunately, some children feel safer when their arousal is higher. A higher state of arousal is 'normal', and regulated is not a state they are used to. This usually occurs when there is a history of poor attachment or trauma. **Some children don't want to 'calm down' because they know that the adult will then leave them alone.** What these children need as a priority is relationship and attachment. There is more information on this in Chapter 2.

Teacher perspective – Dr Emma Goodall

In schools, **when children and young people will not engage in their sensory strategies, it can also be because they are in survival mode,** and as such, the reptilian (snake brain as Kim refers to it) and survival (rat) parts of their brain are in control to ensure they stay alive. In this state, young people are unable to think clearly or make choices or control their behaviour. This behaviour may present as internalizing or externalizing in the school context.

Internalizing behaviour may go unnoticed as these children are quiet and withdrawn, participating minimally if at all, whereas externalizing behaviours are obvious, often resulting in meltdowns or suspensions/exclusions of the young person. It can be scary to see a student externalizing in survival mode, particularly if you do not know this is what it is. When chairs are being thrown or tables overturned, that child cannot engage in anything else. **Not won't, can't.**

Schools may be familiar with the term **meltdown**, often used to describe these high-level externalizing behaviours that are exhibited when an autistic child is in biological/neurological overload/survival mode. Calling this a meltdown implies that this behaviour is intrinsic to the person and there is a perception that it is an autism thing. However, **it is a biological overload/overwhelm thing – think road rage to understand how ubiquitous it is**.

It can be **hard to tell the difference** between a tantrum, which is deliberate and a choice and designed to try and manipulate the situation to get your own way, and survival behaviours (meltdown). One of the easy ways to tell them apart when they are high level is if the young person does or does not destroy their own things while damaging the property around them in general. If they **do not touch their treasured project while destroying everything else**, it is most likely a **tantrum**, whereas if **their things are also damaged**, it is most likely that they are in **survival mode**. In this state, young people need to be left alone, in a safe monitored space, until they are calmer, and then the sensory strategies can be provided to enable them to fully calm down.

Chapter 6

Supporting Self-Regulation

'*Self-regulation is skill.*'

In this chapter, I will explore how to **help children use sensory strategies successfully**. It takes time for children to be able to self-regulate. You should also remember from Chapter 2 that co-regulation is the first step. Some children need more support to **identify their arousal states**. Others need help to **use the correct strategies** to support their arousal.

If you are using a programme which teaches children self-regulation skills, it is highly recommended that this programme is **embedded across the school**. This will provide consistency for both children and staff. It also sends the message that everyone is responsible for helping to support regulation. Programmes can also be used at home, but parents typically benefit from support from either therapists or educators to help set them up.

A note on terminology: body sensations, feelings and emotions

The term '**feeling**' can refer to both a body sensation and an emotion. For example, when someone asks how you are feeling, you might say you have a headache, or you could say you are excited. The first is a body sensation, the second is an emotion.

Body sensations refer to the sensations that can be felt in the body when arousal changes. If you are asking about this it is helpful to ask 'What is your body feeling?' so that children understand that this is different from specific emotions.

Emotion refers to the emotional labels which are given to body sensations.

For example, when experiencing the *emotion* excitement, you might *feel* the *body sensation* of butterflies in your stomach and a lot of energy in your body. At another time, the *body sensation* of butterflies in the stomach could indicate the *emotion* of worry. But a *sensation* of pain in your stomach might indicate that you're *hungry* or *constipated*.

Note from Kim

I am not usually one for semantics. However, **being able to separate body sensations from emotional labels is important** when teaching children how to monitor and manage their own arousal. Before children can correctly label an emotion, they need to be able to sense it. They also need to learn the nuances between those sensations.

Children with **language processing difficulties** often find it hard to label emotions, and describing how their body feels is often much easier for them. Some children are not aware of how their body feels, so this is where their understanding of arousal needs to start. As they progress, using colours and numbers can be a great way to support the labelling of arousal states, without the need for specific emotional language which they may take longer to learn.

Co-regulation comes first

As outlined in Chapter 2, **co-regulation is the start!** It is very difficult for children to learn to self-regulate, if they have not had help to manage their arousal from the adults around them initially. It is incredibly important to remember this.

It is also important that **the adults supporting children to regulate are regulated themselves first**. You must think about your own arousal state before you support the child. It's like the safety message you hear on aeroplanes: 'Put your own mask on first, before helping others.' Supporting regulation is the same. **If you are highly stressed, or annoyed**, it will be much **harder** for you to help a child who is stressed or annoyed to calm down. If your energy is very low, it will harder for you to increase a child's arousal. To help with your own regulation, **you might even want to create your own sensory diet!**

If a child has a history of trauma or neglect, or if there is instability at home, it can be helpful to allocate a **key attachment figure**. This is a specific person whom the child knows they can check in with. Often it is their classroom teacher, but it can also be a classroom assistant or another staff member who is accessible. Initially, it helps if the person checks in with the child daily; this could be in the morning or at another allocated time in the day. Over time, this could be reduced to weekly. The child should also be able to check in with the adult when they need additional support. It is also helpful to keep the attachment figure the same when the child transitions to a new class. If this is not possible, the new key attachment figure should be introduced to the child in the term before they transition so they are familiar with them.

The steps to self-regulation

Before a child can use sensory strategies independently, **they need to be aware of their own arousal state**. This means the child must notice and process every sensory message they are receiving. Dr Emma Goodall (2021) has identified five steps to achieving interoceptive awareness. I think these steps are relevant for all senses and create the foundation for teaching self-regulation.

The steps start with noticing the sensation and finish with managing the implications of the sensation. They serve as a reminder that we can't just expect a child to choose a strategy. If the child doesn't notice the change in their arousal, they won't be able to successfully select the right support strategy.

Step 1: Noticing

First, the child needs **to notice that the body sensation is occurring**. At this stage, they might not know what it means, they may not be able to name it, but they have noticed something has happened. They have noticed that something is different. Maybe their tummy feels strange, or their head hurts.

Step 2: Naming feelings/sensations

At the naming stage, the child learns **to describe the body sensation or what they have noticed**. This includes naming the sensation and labelling where it is. For example, 'my tummy feels sore', or 'my tummy feels as if I need to use the toilet'.

Step 3: Linking emotions/arousal state

Next, we learn **to attach an emotion to the sensation**. Sometimes, there might not be a specific emotion. For example, if we are at home and need the toilet, we will just go to the toilet. However, if we are out walking in a field and need to use the toilet, but don't know where the toilet is, depending on how desperately we need the toilet, we might start to feel anxious.

Dr Goodall's original work does not specifically mention **arousal state**. I add it in here because I have worked with **a lot of children who struggle with their emotional vocabulary**. Initially these children may not be able to label a specific emotion. **Teaching them about high and low arousal gives them a structure that they can use to start to label the feelings they are having.** It helps them to identify if their arousal is high or low, and, in the case of the arousal bar, comfortable or uncomfortable. For example, they might identify worried as a yellow three.

Using colours, and then colours and numbers, gives these children a starting point. It helps them to **learn about their arousal state without needing specific vocabulary for feelings or emotions.** This lets them begin to understand the impact of arousal and to choose support strategies without the explicit vocabulary they find harder to learn at first. It also provides **an easier strategy when children's arousal is high**. If you remember, at this time they have less access to their thinking brain, so have much less access to the language centre. 'Red' is often easier to get out than 'angry or frustrated'.

Using colours also allows adults to label arousal without mislabelling emotions. Sometimes we can see a change in arousal state, but we might not know what is triggering it. This means we might label the feeling incorrectly. Using colours and numbers will avoid this and help the child to articulate what they are feeling themselves.

Step 4: Understanding impact
Understanding the impact requires forward thinking, planning and reflection. So, if a child is playing with their toys and ignores the feeling of needing the toilet, they will learn that this means they might wet themselves. The impact of ignoring the interoceptive sensations is that the bladder eventually just releases the urine. Or, for those us who get hangry, the impact might be that we lose our temper at something quite minor.

Step 5: Managing
Managing is the final step. **Here we use our interoceptive awareness to act.** For the child who got the interoceptive messages about needing

the toilet, manging this would involve stopping playing and going to the toilet. The hangry person needs to stop what they are doing and go and eat. As we gain even more interoceptive awareness, we can take pro-active management steps.

For example, if you know that leaving your assignment to the last minute will result in significant anxiety, you might plan to do it the week before. Or, if you know that your child might find assembly overwhelming, you might plan for them to attend for a shorter time – and you could ensure that they have done some calming and regulating activities before and after they attend.

Learn more

Watch Dr Goodall's YouTube video on the steps to interoceptive awareness. It is at the bottom of this page: www.griffinot.com/interoception-explained

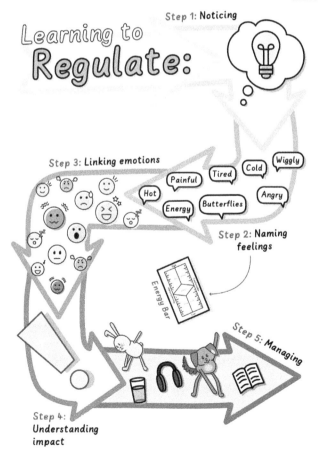

Learning to self-regulate

Co-regulation teaches children these steps. Initially, the adult does the steps for the child. For example, if a baby has a wet nappy, the caregiver will usually feel it, and then say something like: 'Your nappy is wet. I can see you're upset, let me change it and that will make it better.' The caregiver is walking the child through each of the regulation steps.

If the child has the ability to **attend to and process this information**, they are learning the skills they need to self-regulate when they are older. As their brains develop through the toddler and teenage years their skills will mature. They will need support at the start, and if they are completely dysregulated, but eventually the child will achieve independence. As an adult, it will be their turn to co-regulate other children.

When children have language, social communication or learning delays, they may not be able to process these cues from their caregivers as infants. This means they will need **more support** to learn to self-regulate when they are older. It is important to have support from the child's speech and language therapist (and psychologist if they have one) to ensure that they are able to access the curriculum you are using to teach self-regulation.

Sometimes, a child does not receive this support from their caregiver. This means they will need more support to develop self-regulation. These children typically benefit the most from a key attachment figure.

Note from Kim

If you are reading this book, it is likely you are working with children who have poor self-regulation skills. **Your role is to support them to understand each of the steps.** It is hugely important that you don't just expect a child to be able to manage using a support strategy they have been given. You must help them to understand when their body will need the strategy and what it feels like when their body doesn't.

Isla self-regulates

Isla experiences sound sensitivity in the classroom. She needs to notice that it is loud, identify that that is not comfortable for her and understand that if she doesn't take steps she will probably shut down. To avoid hiding under her desk, she can put on a pair of ear defenders.

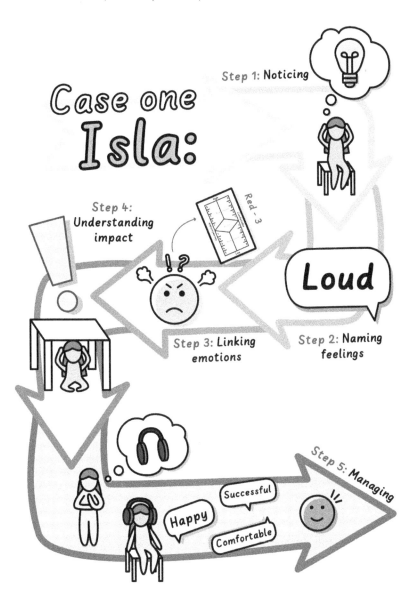

Noah self-regulates

Noah is rocking on his chair. He notices that his body is feeling wiggly and he's rocking. He realizes that his arousal is too low to focus, which means he won't get his work done. He chooses to go to the Move it Zone to increase his arousal level.

Tools that help in the classroom

There are several **commercially available** tools that can help you to teach self-regulation to your class. The most successful way is to have a **whole-school approach**. Instead of just teaching the tools to specific students or groups of students, the approach should be taught to all classes. It should also **be included within the school's behaviour policy as a de-escalation strategy**. This will mean that all staff are using the same language and they understand the language the child is using. It also creates consistency for children when they move class.

The tools below are identified as either **linear or circular**. **Linear models** teach arousal using a **single dimension of high to low**. They are a straight line. They do not separate out comfortable and uncomfortable feelings within high and low arousal states. The Alert® Programme and the Zones of Regulation® are both examples of linear models.

Circular, or circumferential, models have two dimensions, and look more like a circle. The first dimension, or axis, like linear models, is high and low. **The second dimension or axis separates comfortable and uncomfortable.** These could also be called pleasant and unpleasant arousal states. The arousal bar presented in Chapter 2 is an example of a circular model.

Benefits of using a circular model

The concept of a circumferential model to categorize emotions was explored in depth by James A. Russell in 1980. His initial work categorized core emotions into a circular order.

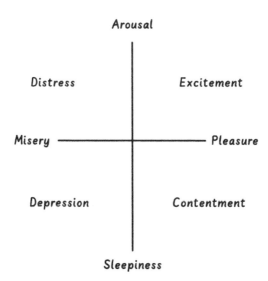

A circular model helps children to identify that their arousal can increase, and decrease, but in different ways. Sometimes this increase occurs because something enjoyable has happened, for example they might have just had an ice-cream! However, sometimes an increase occurs because something unpleasant has happened. It is the same with lower arousal, sometimes it is because you are calm and content, but other times it is because you are sad.

This distinction is important as the child may need to use different strategies to regulate depending on why their arousal state has changed. If their arousal is lower because they are calm, they might not need a strategy. But if it is lower because something upset them, they might need support from an adult. On a **linear model**, these feelings would fall into the same colour, which makes it harder for children to identify strategies. It also makes it more difficult for children who have greater understanding as they struggle to understand why such different emotions are all grouped together.

Practical example

I remember working with an eight-year-old boy who very **quickly understood** colour concepts of the Zones of Regulation, a linear model. He looked perplexed by yellow and red. He **could not understand why frustrated and excited were together in yellow** and **why angry and elated went together in red**. He understood that these feelings increased energy in his body, but he was able to explain quite frankly **that they were completely different feelings!** After experiencing this confusion in children time and time again while using the Zones of Regulation, when I can choose the model, these days I primarily teach arousal using a circular model of emotions.

Learn more

Russell explores the concept further in an article he wrote with colleagues which is published in *Development and Psychopathology* (Posner, Russell & Peterson 2005). It's called 'The circumplex model of affect: An integrative approach to affective neuroscience, cognitive development, and psychopathology'. You can read it here: https://doi. org/10.1017/S0954579405050340

Teacher perspective – Dr Emma Goodall

In many instances, **teachers do not have much choice about what sensory tools they use in the classroom** because these school-wide decisions have already been made by school leadership. In these cases, where the tools are not meeting the needs of all the students, it is important for educators to gather information about the gaps that they can identify between support needs and strategy provision.

These gaps can be **context based**: think no clear markings and spaces in a school with a couple of students with visual impairments, or open-plan classrooms for noise-sensitive autistic students or students with ADHD. Alternatively, these gaps can be **skills based or developmental gaps**. For example, if the majority of the class are able to be co-regulated easily and are well on their way to being able to self-regulate, the few students that are unable to notice, recognize or respond helpfully to their emotions and feelings are less likely to be supported effectively than if they were in a class where no one had those skills yet due to their developmental profile.

Whole-class and whole-school strategies are a much **more compassionate way to address skills-based gaps** as they do not single out particular students as being 'behind' or 'less skilled' than their peers. It is important to **look at tools that are available to see if they will make sense to your cohort of students**. Many neurodiverse students need a basic foundation of interoception building before other tools are used, which means that if you choose a tool that is based on the students having developed their interoception already, no matter how good the tool is, it won't support those students effectively.

In addition, if students are **culturally and linguistically diverse** it is important to think about the appropriateness of tools, especially if they are teaching about the expression of feelings and emotions. This is because **different cultures have different norms relating to emotional expression**. Think about some people who talk loudly and use large body movements to express excitement and contrast this with some people who maintain a neutral facial expression and tone of voice at all times. It can be helpful to discuss these issues as a whole staff and/or with an occupational therapist who is familiar with your student cohort.

Tools that are available

While the list that follows includes all commercially available programmes I am currently aware of, this does not mean it is exhaustive. A quick description and the pros and cons of each will be given. Tools are listed in alphabetical order.

Just one note on terminology – when I use the term lesson plans, I am referring to a full set of lesson resources which can be used in the classroom to teach the concepts. The tools with lesson plans have weekly teaching resources in their manuals. The amount of preparation teachers will need to do varies. The term scheme of work is often used in the UK to describe what I am referring to.

Alert® programme – linear model

Available from: www.alertprogram.com

The Alert® programme is the oldest self-regulation programme I am aware of. It was published in 1990. The authors are North American. The programme uses the analogy of a car to describe their linear model. There is some teaching guidance, but not a complete set of lesson plans. The book focuses heavily on arousal levels and sensory strategies to help to change arousal level.

PROS

- Online training is available

- Research demonstrates effectiveness

- Provides regulation strategy ideas

CONS

- Resources are dated: the book has not been updated since it was first printed in 1990

- Programme does not link arousal to emotions

- Language may need adapting for children with language disorders

- Curriculum needs to be adapted for younger children

- Lesson plans need to be created from the teaching guidance in the book

Feel It Change It – circular model

Available from: www.griffinot.com/feel-it-change-it

Feel It Change It is designed by Kim and was developed in the UK. It uses the arousal bar to teach regulation. As children develop greater understanding, the bar opens into a circle which helps them to understand that multiple emotions can be felt at the same time. For example, excited and worried would become an orange feeling, a combination of yellow and red.

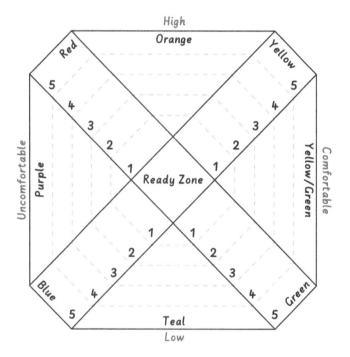

The Feel It Change It lesson plans are broken into three sections. These are designed to be taught over time, at the pace the children need. The first section explores arousal and how children can change their level of arousal. The second section progresses to using vocabulary to describe feelings and emotions. The final section considers the impact of our arousal states and teaches children the neurology that underpins them. All sections provide children with strategies they can use to regulate.

Feel It Change It is a complete package which includes training, lesson plans and teaching resources. The lessons require very little preparation and include videos to teach children the concepts. It is available for schools to purchase on an annual subscription that gives ongoing access to the resources. It includes access to content for parents to use at home.

PROS

- Staff and parent training (online)
- Teaching materials for lesson plans are provided, including videos
- Designed for children from four years old
- Differentiation for children with language and communication delays
- Access to group coaching support for staff
- Includes emotional vocabulary and neurological responses as children progress
- Provides regulation support ideas and teaches children how to use them

CONS

- Initially more complex to teach
- Ongoing annual subscription to access teaching resources

Interoceptive Curriculum – linear model

Available from: www.kelly-mahler.com

The Interoceptive Curriculum is written by North American occupational therapist Kelly Mahler. It is a complete programme designed to teach children how their interoceptive system impacts their behaviour and responses. The programme initially focuses on identifying how the body, including the internal organs, feels. It then considers emotions and strategies to support regulation.

PROS

- Manual with 25 lesson plans and additional resources
- Training is available

- Great physical activities to help with labelling body feelings

CONS

- Only considers interoception

Ready to Learn Interoceptive Toolkit – linear model

Available from: https://www.education.sa.gov.au/schools-and-educators/curriculum-and-teaching/curriculum-programs/applying-interoception-skills-classroom

The interoceptive toolkit is a free resource published by the South Australia Department of Education. It was written by Dr Emma Goodall, who has been writing the teacher's perspective sections of this book. Her work outlines the five steps to interoceptive awareness you read about earlier in this chapter. The toolkit includes lesson resources that teach children the steps from noticing through to choosing a strategy.

PROS

- Free resource

- Lesson plans and resources

CONS

- Only considers interoception

- Limited training

- No consideration of emotions or other senses

RULER – circular model

Available from: www.rulerapproach.org

Book: *Permission to Feel: Unlock the Power of Emotions to Help Yourself and Your Child Thrive* by Marc A. Brackett (2019, Celadon Books & Quercus)

The RULER approach has been developed by Dr Marc Brackett who is based at Yale. It is a circular model which focuses on emotional intelligence. RULER stands for recognizing, understanding, labelling, expressing and regulating. The steps are similar to the five identified by Dr Goodall as outlined above.

RULER is a whole-school initiative. It includes staff training and the tools required to teach children the RULER principles at school. The programme includes a colour/number grid and a significant amount of emotional vocabulary.

PROS

- Considers all dimensions of arousal and links this directly to emotions

- Extremely thorough theoretical model behind the programme

- Good research supporting its outcomes

- Access to online platform that includes resources, virtual coaching and support webinars

CONS

- Training is expensive and must be completed before schools gain access to the online platform

- RULER is language heavy and may need to be adapted for children with language or cognition delays

Sensory Ladders – linear model

Available from: https://sensoryladders.org

Sensory Ladders were developed by UK-based occupational therapist Kath Smith. Kath uses a ladder to explain how arousal increases and decreases. Children are encouraged to identify how they feel at each arousal state using both words and pictures. Each child creates their own sensory ladder using the words and images that have meaning to them. For example, a child might use animals to show how their arousal states change, with turtle being slow and lion being high arousal.

PROS

- Free online training for professionals and parents

- Simple to use

- Very flexible and can be adapted to match children's needs and preferences

- Can be used with any age

CONS

- Does not specifically teach emotional vocabulary

- No manual

- No lesson plans for teaching groups

Shanker Self-Reg®

Available from: https://self-reg.ca

Books: *Self-Reg Schools: A Handbook for Educators* by Dr Stuart Shanker & Susan Hopkins (2019 Penguin Publishing); *Self-Reg: How to Help Your Child (and You) Break the Stress Cycle and Successfully Engage with Life* by Dr Stuart Shanker (2016, Penguin Publishing)

Self-Reg® has been created primarily in Canada by Dr Stuart Shanker. The programme explores the neurological response to stress and how this impacts behaviour, learning and well-being. There is a focus on training staff to see past behaviour and consider how they respond to children's stresses in a pro-active way. The model doesn't label arousal or emotions specifically. The process outlined in Self-Reg® is to reframe behaviour, recognize the stress which caused the behaviour to occur, reduce the stress, improve stress awareness and restore energy. **It is primarily aimed at changing the adult's behaviour and responses so that they can support their children.**

PROS

- Training provides very clear information on the development of self-regulation and how this impacts behaviour

- Strong links between regulation and learning

- Strong focus on well-being

- Focus on reframing behaviour to focus on the underlying stressors and arousal needs of the child

- Training and books explain how to implement Self-Reg® and include tools

- Additional supports for parents

CONS

- Does not include specific lesson plans, but is designed more specifically to teach staff how to change their interactions

- Language and cognitive processing are heavy, so will require adapting for children with additional needs

- While thorough, it is more complex than other tools, making it harder to implement

- Helpful to have a multi-disciplinary team to implement the programme

- High cost and time required to complete the full training

The Zones of Regulation – linear model

Available from: www.zonesofregulation.com

(The book is also usually available on Amazon)

The Zones of Regulation is a linear model which breaks arousal into four colours. Each colour represents increasing or decreasing arousal. There are emotions linked to each colour as well. The book provides a complete lesson plan/scheme of work that schools can use to teach arousal and emotional regulation to children in schools. There are suggested resources and activities for each lesson.

PROS

- Widely used, so staff and students moving between schools may have already used it

- Staff training available online and in person (mostly in the USA)

- Straightforward to implement

- Numerous additional resources on the website and on many other websites (including Twinkl)

CONS

- Original lesson plans, presented in the book, need to be heavily adapted for younger students and students with special educational needs and disabilities

- Without training, there is a danger of staff expecting children to be 'green' all the time without fully understanding regulation concepts

- Grouping of positive and negative emotions together can be confusing for students and doesn't allow for developing an understanding of more complex emotions

Once you have chosen a tool

It is important to **set aside time to plan how you will implement the tool in your school**. Some of the tools will require staff training and this will need to be scheduled into your continuing professional development (CPD) schedule. Most tools require resources to be created, and this will also take time. You should also consider how you monitor student progress when using the tool.

It is helpful for staff who will be using the tool to have training. As a minimum, it is recommended that they have read some information on arousal and regulation, including the basic neurology. Essentially, they should be aware of the fundamental concepts discussed in Chapters 1–3 of this book. Most of the available tools have specific training available, and since 2020 this includes online options. Budget and CPD time will need to be allocated for training.

Next, it's helpful to make **a clear plan** of what regulation supports, both sensory and non-sensory, can be used in your setting. This will require an audit of available equipment, staff and space. Depending on the tools and equipment that you already have, you may need to allocate some budget for training and purchasing equipment. Space may also need to be allocated. For example, the hall each morning for a sensory circuit, or a small room as the designated calm zone. While supports should be individualized, it is helpful to have consistency with visuals and general strategies; for example, every classroom has a 'Move it Zone' which uses the same cards.

It is highly recommended that you have **a risk assessment in place for equipment**, especially things like scooter boards and weighted blankets. There should be an equipment maintenance and cleaning plan. All staff should be made aware of these. It can be helpful to have a system of recording where equipment is.

Finally, **the teaching time needs to be scheduled into the class timetable**. It might be that one teacher is responsible for delivering the lessons, or that all teachers are trained to do this. General concepts could be taught in assembly with follow-up tasks being completed in class. Each school is different and will need to work out the best plan for them.

Additional resources

Kim's online training Sensory Aware with GriffinOT discusses risk assessments and provides templates for these. Learn more: www.griffinot.com

Reflective practice

- ♦ Which of the tools would be the most relevant for your setting and why?

- ♦ What sensory supports are realistic for you to implement in your setting?

Appendix

Additional resources are also available on the GriffinOT website https://GriffinOT.com/success. The accompanying section can be downloaded from https://library.jkp.com/redeem using the code VYASPAL.

★ ## Screening checklist
Part 1: Child's perspective
If the child is able to contribute, consider each of the senses with the child and what their preferences are.

	I find this easy/I enjoy	I find this tricky/I don't enjoy
Taste		
Smell		
Sounds/Noises		
Sights		
Touch		
Body awareness		
Balance/Movement		
Doing my work		

Part 2: Arousal contributors
EXTERNAL FACTORS

1. Environment sensations: Use the environmental checklist to help your analysis.

- In which environments is the child successful?

- Which environments are more challenging?

2. People: Consider relationships between adults and peers, and both positive and negative influencing factors.

    - Which relationships support the child?

    - Which relationships are more challenging?

3. Tasks and activities.

    - With which tasks is the child successful?

    - Which tasks do they find more challenging?

Are there any other external stressors (e.g., new sibling, sick parents, unstable housing, exam period)?

INTERNAL FACTORS

1. Is the child aware of their internal body sensations? Can they manage these successfully?

2. What is the child's sleep like?

3. Are there any internal stressors (e.g., personal expectations, perfectionism)?

4. What motivates the child to succeed?

5. Is there a diagnosis that needs to be considered?

6. Do communication skills need to be considered?

HISTORY

1. Cumulative sensations: Consider what has occurred beforehand and the sensations across the day.

2. Previous experiences: Consider any previous experiences that might be impacting the child's participation and engagement.

3. Are there any adverse childhood experiences (e.g., trauma, neglect, poverty)?

Part 3: Sensory reactivity

Taste

Sensitive	Slow	Seeking
• Only eats familiar foods • Prefers bland foods • Dislikes strong-tasting mints or candies • Gags when new foods are presented	• Often doesn't notice or care whether food is spicy or bland	• Adds salt and spice to food • Prefers spicy food • Puts objects into their mouth prior to playing with them

Smell

Sensitive	Slow	Seeking
• Dislikes fragrances from perfume or bath products • Shows distress at smells that other children do not notice • Finds smells in a restaurant or school lunch hall difficult • Requests to leave store or a space with strong smells	• Is unable to distinguish between different smells • Doesn't notice noxious (dangerous or offensive) smells	• Smells people, animals and objects • Enjoys being close to people who wear perfume or cologne

Vision

Sensitive	Slow	Seeking
• Dislikes bright lights or sunshine (blinks, squints, closes eyes) • Becomes distressed in unusual visual environments (e.g., bright colourful room, wall decorations) • Prefers to work in low lighting • Bothered by fast-moving images on TV/film • Prefers having the shades down/curtains closed • Is easily distracted visually • Likes wearing hats, caps or sunglasses	• Seems oblivious to details of an object and the surrounding environment (including signs) • Doesn't notice if others walk into a room • Needs help to find objects that are obvious to others • Walks into objects or people as if they were not there	• Watches visually stimulating scenes (e.g., aquarium, spinning objects) • Chooses objects that are brightly coloured, including clothing • Likes to flip light switches on and off • Likes bright lights • Enjoys looking at movement of objects out of the corner of his or her eyes

Auditory (Sound/Noise)

Sensitive	Slow	Seeking
• Dislikes loud, unexpected sounds (sirens, school bells) • Responds negatively to loud noises by running away, crying or holding hands over ears • Startles easily to unexpected sounds • Prefers to stay away from noisy settings • Is easily distracted by background noises such as a lawn mower outside, an air conditioner, a refrigerator or buzz from fluorescent lights • Is distracted by background noise such as TV/radio when trying to work • Fears music concerts or cinema or assembly/lunch hall (cafeteria) • Has difficulty with higher pitched sounds such as hand driers and vacuum cleaners	• Does not respond when his or her name is called • Does not respond to instructions given once • May not hear sounds in the environment • May appear to be in own world • May not be able to tell the direction sound has come from • Asks 'what' frequently • May make their own noises for fun	• Loves to play music and television at extremely loud volumes • Makes noise in the background while doing other tasks* • Enjoys noisy environments such as sports stadiums/arenas, shopping centres/malls and the cinema

* Consider if this is to drown out other sounds

Tactile (Touch)

Sensitive	Slow	Seeking*
• Dislikes having messy hands • Dislikes having hair cut/brushed • Has difficulty with toe and fingernail cutting • Is fussy with food textures • Pulls away from being lightly touched or hugged • Seems bothered when someone touches his or her face (light kiss) • Dislikes teeth brushing more than others • Feels anxious when standing close to others, e.g., in line • Is sensitive to certain fabrics/new clothes • Is irritated by certain clothing textures, labels and seams and socks, and avoids new clothes • Is irritated by shoes • Has difficulty at the dentist	• Doesn't notice if hands or face are messy or dirty • Doesn't cry when seriously hurt and isn't bothered by minor injuries • Doesn't notice when someone touches him or her • Has an unusually high tolerance for pain • Is unaware of temperature changes • May not notice if bumped or pushed	• Touches and feels objects • Touches people to the point of irritating them • Puts things in their mouth; licking, sucking, chewing (hair, pencils, clothing, doorknobs) • Seeks out vibration • Loves messy play • Likes haircuts

* Consider if the child is compensating for reduced proprioceptive awareness

Proprioception (Body awareness)

Sensitive	Slow	Seeking*
• No report in literature	• Becomes tired easily, especially when standing or holding the body in one position • Leans on walls or slumps on furniture • Uses too much force, and can often break things as a result • Walks loudly, as if feet are heavy • Often described as having 'weak muscles'	• Pushes, pulls, hanging off things • Jumps and crashes around • Chews on items • Cracks knuckles • Grinds teeth • Likes tight-fitting clothing

* Consider if the child is using the proprioceptive input to help to reduce their arousal due to overload from another sense

Vestibular (Movement)

Sensitive	Slow	Seeking
• Avoids playing on swings and slides (either now or when younger) • Has a fear of heights • Dislikes having feet off the ground • Seems afraid of riding in lifts or on escalators • Avoids having head tipped back (e.g., when washing hair) • Dislikes being moved by someone else • Prefers sedentary activities • Has difficulty learning to ride a bike • Becomes travel sick or dizzy easily	• Bumps into things or falls over objects • May prefer sedentary activities like computer time to active physical games • Loses balance unexpectedly when walking on an uneven surface • Often has poor muscle tone (appears more floppy than others) • Has slow motor responses • Tires quickly/has poor endurance	• Jumps and crashes around • Moves by spinning and rolling! • Shows a strong preference for excessive spinning, swinging or rolling • Takes excessive risks during play (e.g., climbs high into trees, jumps off tall furniture) • Pursues movement to the point it interferes with daily routines • Rocks in chair on floor or while standing • Jumps on bed or sofa excessively • Loves extreme fast-moving input (e.g., swings/slides/rollercoaster) • Rarely gets dizzy

Interoception

Consider the following.

Does the child recognize when they:

- are hungry?
- feel full?
- are thirsty?
- are hot?
- are cold?
- need to go to the toilet?
- are tired?
- are too excited?
- are stressed/worried?
- are feeling sick?
- are becoming unwell?

Do they:

- ask for/get food when hungry?
- ask for/get a drink when thirsty?
- take off/put on their jumper if hot/cold?
- make it to the toilet with sufficient time (i.e., not at the last minute)?
- rest when they are tired?
- identify subtle changes in their emotions (e.g., when they are a little annoyed)?
- speak to adults if they are stressed/worried?
- advise adults when they are feeling sick/unwell?

Part 4: Praxis/Posture

Dyspraxia		
Ideation	Planning	Doing
• Cannot think of ideas for play/stories/writing • Is repetitive with play • Doesn't start an activity • Watches others first before they start	• Has ideas, but moves on and doesn't start the activity, so looks inattentive • Has difficulty learning *new tasks*, including routines, steps, sports, daily activities • Has difficulty completing tasks with several steps • Has poor organization of materials and self • Doesn't generalize learning from one situation to another • Prefers fantasy games or talking to actually doing things	• Takes longer to do things • Is clumsy and accident prone • Trips up or bumps into people or things • Has difficulty with hopping, jumping, skipping or running compared to same-aged peers • Has poor skills in ball activities or other sports • Has difficulty with fine motor activities like buttons, writing and using scissors • Is untidy when eating • Prefers sedentary activities
Postural control		
• Seems weaker than other children their age • Has a loose grasp on objects • Has difficulty turning handles or taps that require some pressure • Has poor balance during motor activities and may fall over easily, sometimes even when seated • Has difficulty using both hands at the same time and may not consistently use their non-dominant hand to help • Tires easily or appears tired most of the time • May appear lazy or unmotivated and prefer sedentary activities		

You can download a printable version of this checklist here: https://library.jkp.com/redeem.

★ Environmental checklist

Environment being assessed: Main classroom   Lunch hall   PE hall
Playground   Corridor   Other classroom/space:

Child's perspective – prompt for each sense if needed

Are there any sensations you find helpful in this room/space?

Are there any sensations you find distracting or tricky to manage in this room/space?

Smell		
Check for	**Notes**	**Changes required**
Cleaning scents		
Air fresheners		
Food smells • Kitchen cooking • Lunchboxes		
Staff/peers • Deodorants/ perfumes • Shampoo • Laundry detergent		
Plant scents, e.g., flowers		
Animal smells, e.g., pets		

Vision		
Check for	**Notes**	**Changes required**
Lighting • Flickering • Intensity if sitting under		
Reflections • Windows/shiny surfaces		
Distractions • Wall displays • Shadows/sunlight • Outdoor activity/ object • Preferred object • Clutter		

Sound		
Check for	**Notes**	**Changes required**
Overall noise level • Staff • Children • Other sounds, e.g., traffic, music room, corridor noise		
Electrical equipment • Projectors • Screens/TV • Air conditioner/fan/ heater		
Intrusive/unexpected sounds • Printer printing • School bell/whistles • Gardener		
Echoes/Acoustics • From children within class • From other classes		

Touch		
Check for	**Notes**	**Changes required**
Space around the child • Air vents/fan • Proximity of others • Being bumped into		
Clothing, e.g., uniform • Fabrics • Tightness • Flexibility		
Staff/peer interactions • Warn before touching		
Tricky textures • Glue/tape • Feel of pencil/paper • Feel of desk/chair		

Proprioceptive (if relevant)		
Check for	**Notes**	**Changes required**
Space around the child • Proximity of others		
Movement opportunities • Heavy work • Movement breaks		
Seating • Support for body awareness		

Vestibular (if relevant)		
Check for	**Notes**	**Changes required**
Space around the child • Proximity of others		
Movement opportunities • Movement breaks		
Seating • Consider dynamic options • Consider sensitivity		
Sensitivity • Uneven surfaces • Unstable surfaces • Height, e.g., stage/ platform		

General		
Check for	**Notes**	**Changes required**
Child's position in room • Away from specific distractions • Consider sensory fit of peers in space		
Access to regulation strategies • Proximity to supports • Staff to implement supports		

You can download a printable version of this checklist here: https://library.jkp.com/redeem.

★ Sensory passport

My name:		
My goals:		
My sensory preferences:		My sensory triggers:
My communication supports:		
My arousal		
Arousal	I look like	This helps
0		
Red 3		
Yellow 3		
Blue 3		
Green 3		
S = I can do this independently. **H** = I need help.		

You can download a printable version of this passport here: https://library.jkp.com/redeem.

Case Study 1: Isla

Isla is a six-year-old autistic girl. At school she finds it difficult to block out the whirring of the projector and the ticking of the clock. These background noises increase her level of arousal throughout the day. She must work harder to calm her body down (decrease her arousal) and focus on her teacher. The PE hall is extremely hard for her to stay calm in because the sounds echo and significantly increase her level of arousal. She had never engaged in messy play and dislikes art because of the sticky textures like glue and tape. She struggles with certain clothing fabrics, including her school uniform.

Screening checklist: Isla
Part 1: Child's perspective

If the child is able to contribute, consider each of the senses with the child and what their preferences are.

	I find this easy/I enjoy	I find this tricky/I don't enjoy
Taste	Ice-cream	
Smell	Flowers	Food smells, especially fish
Sounds/ Noises	Soft music	Loud sounds Clock ticking Whistle/shouting in PE Shouting on playground
Sights		Sunshine
Touch	My fluffy blanket	Glue My socks hurt sometimes Other children touching me

Part 2: Arousal contributors
EXTERNAL FACTORS

1. Environment sensations: Use the environmental checklist to help your analysis.

    • In which environments is the child successful? *Quieter spaces with fewer children.*

    • Which environments are more challenging? *Loud spaces or spaces with a lot of movement around her.*

2. People: Consider relationships between adults and peers, and both positive and negative influencing factors.

    • Which relationships support the child? *Class teacher, class teaching assistant Daniel, librarian, parents, sister Lucie.*

    • Which relationships are more challenging? *Class teaching assistant Sophie.*

3. Tasks and activities.

   - With which tasks is the child successful? *Reading, writing/ literacy, maths, geography.*

   - Which tasks do they find more challenging? *Art, PE, assembly.*

4. Are there any other external stressors (e.g., new sibling, sick parents, unstable housing, exam period)? *Mother travels for work occasionally overnight; this increases Isla's arousal level.*

INTERNAL FACTORS

1. Is the child aware of their internal body sensations? Can they manage these successfully? *Yes, but won't use unfamiliar toilets.*

2. What is the child's sleep like? *Usually okay, disrupted if mother is away.*

3. Are there any internal stressors (e.g., personal expectations, perfectionism)? *Isla's arousal increases if she makes a mistake; she struggles to move on and can sometimes destroy her work.*

4. What motivates the child to succeed? *Isla loves to have time with her dog. She also enjoys spending time in the library and book corner.*

5. Is there a diagnosis that needs to be considered? *Autism.*

6. Do communication skills need to be considered? *Yes, Isla's social communication skills are poor, in line with her autism diagnosis. Her language skills reduce significantly when her arousal is higher. Visual supports are required at this time.*

HISTORY

1. Cumulative sensations: Consider what has occurred beforehand and the sensations across the day. *Days when there are art or PE increase Isla's arousal. Her arousal usually increases two days before her mother leaves, and it takes her a further two days to regulate.*

2. Previous experiences: Consider any previous experiences that might be impacting the child's participation and engagement. *None.*

3. Are there any adverse childhood experiences (e.g., trauma, neglect, poverty)? *No.*

Part 3: Sensory reactivity

Taste		
Sensitive	**Slow**	**Seeking**
• Only eats familiar foods		

Smell		
Sensitive	**Slow**	**Seeking**
• Dislikes fragrances from perfume or bath products • Shows distress at smells that other children do not notice • Finds smells in a restaurant or school lunch hall difficult		

Vision		
Sensitive	**Slow**	**Seeking**
• Becomes distressed in unusual visual environments (e.g., bright, colourful room, wall decorations) • Prefers to work in low lighting		

Auditory (Sound/Noise)		
Sensitive	Slow	Seeking
• Dislikes loud, unexpected sounds (e.g., sirens, school bells) • Responds negatively to loud noises by running away, crying or holding hands over ears • Startles easily to unexpected sounds • Prefers to stay away from noisy settings • Is easily distracted by background noises such as a lawn mower outside, an air conditioner, a refrigerator or buzz from fluorescent lights • Fears music concerts or cinema or assembly/lunch hall (cafeteria)		• Makes noise in the background while doing other tasks*

* Isla does this when the noise around her increases, in an attempt to drown out the other sounds.

Tactile (Touch)		
Sensitive	Slow	Seeking
• Dislikes having messy hands • Is fussy with food textures • Dislikes teeth brushing more than others • Is anxious when standing close to others (e.g., in line) • Is sensitive to certain fabrics/new clothes • Is irritated with certain clothing textures, labels and seams and socks, and avoids new clothes • Is irritated by shoes • Has difficulty at the dentist		

Proprioception (Body awareness)		
Sensitive	Slow	Seeking
		• Chews on items • Likes tight-fitting clothing

Vestibular (Movement)		
Sensitive	Slow	Seeking
• Avoids having head tipped back (e.g., washing hair) • Becomes travel sick or dizzy easily		• Likes jumping and crashing!

INTEROCEPTION

Consider the following.

Does the child recognize when they...? *Yes to all.*

Do they:

- Identify subtle changes in their emotions (e.g., when they are a little annoyed)? *Isla has difficulty with this.*

- Speak to adults if they are stressed/worried? *Sometimes, it depends how high her arousal level is. If it is too high she will shut down rather than seek out help/support.*

- Advise adults when they are feeling sick/unwell? *Yes. Isla treats all tummy upsets as being very sick, but sometimes it is likely that she is feeling anxious.*

Part 4: Praxis/Posture

Dyspraxia		
Ideation	**Planning**	**Doing**
		• Takes longer to do things • Has difficulty with hopping, jumping, skipping or running compared to same-aged peers • Has poor skills in ball activities or other sports

Environmental checklist: Isla
Environment being assessed: Main classroom

Child's perspective – prompt for each sense if needed

Are there any sensations you find helpful in this room/space?

- *I like it when the class is quiet*

Are there any sensations you find distracting or tricky to manage in this room/space?

- *I don't like sitting next to the window when it's open*

- *I don't like being near Oliver because he bumps into me*

Smell		
Check for	**Notes**	**Changes required**
Staff/peers • Deodorants/ perfumes • Shampoo • Laundry detergent	Some staff wear strong perfumes	Change uniform policy to request staff use unscented deodorants and avoid perfume

Vision		
Check for	**Notes**	**Changes required**
Distractions • Wall displays • Shadows/sunlight • Outdoor activity/object • Preferred object • Clutter	Isla reports some visual sensory overload when there are a lot of colours on the wall displays	Use a maximum of three colours on displays Displays will only be on the back walls of the room

Sounds		
Check for	**Notes**	**Changes required**
Overall noise level • Staff • Children • Other sounds (e.g., traffic, music room, corridor noise)	Teacher has a 'noiseometer' in the classroom which indicates when children are too loud and aims to keep classroom noise as low as possible	Continue to use 'noiseometer' Make ear defenders available as well
Electrical equipment • Projectors • Screens/TV • Air conditioner, fan, heater	There is a whirr from the projector	Seat Isla at desks that are the furthest away from the projector Turn off projector when not in use
Intrusive/unexpected sounds • Printer printing • School bell/whistles • Gardener	Staff use a whistle in the playground to end play	Staff member to let Isla know in advance so she knows when the whistle will be blown
Echoes/Acoustics • From children within class • From other classes	Some chairs are missing sliders, which makes them loud when moved	Replace sliders on chairs

Touch		
Check for	**Notes**	**Changes required**
Space around the child • Air vents/fan • Proximity of others • Being bumped into	Isla noted she does not like the feel of breeze from the window or air vent She also identified that Oliver often bumps into her	Seat Isla at desks away from the window and air vent Seat Isla away from Oliver
Clothing (e.g., uniform) • Fabrics • Tightness • Flexibility	Isla's mother has found seam-free/soft fabrics for her school uniform Isla does not have to wear the school tie She can wear black trainers instead of school shoes	
Staff/peer interactions • Warn before touching		Remind all staff at next staff meeting of Isla's needs
Tricky textures • Glue/tape • Feel of pencil/paper • Feel of desk/chair	Isla struggles with glue/tape, she has support from the classroom assistant for these activities	

General		
Check for	**Notes**	**Changes required**
Child's position in room • Away from specific distractions • Consider sensory fit of peers in space	Consider proximity to Oliver	
Access to regulation strategies • Proximity to supports • Staff to implement supports	Current quiet space is far from her classroom	Consider proximity to quiet space for classroom allocation next academic year

Sensory planning: Isla
Reviewing the evaluation documents and information
Isla experiences sensitivities with her auditory and touch senses. These impact her ability to participate in activities like art, PE and assembly. She will overload when there is too much sensory information, particularly with sound. When this occurs, she does not participate in class, she will hide under her desk or in the toilet. Isla is not joining in for assembly or music as she finds them too overwhelming. There are some changes that need to be made to the environment.

Changes to her uniform have already been agreed with her parents. Isla's mother has reported that she is starting to say she doesn't want to come to school, and she arrives late two to three times a week. She is at risk of becoming a school refuser.

Goal setting
The primary goal for Isla is to help lower her arousal across the day to allow her to stay engaged at school.

CURRENT GOALS

1. Isla will access sensory supports to lower her arousal 50 per cent of the time when she becomes overloaded in the classroom.

2. Isla will come into school 90 per cent of the time without complaint in the morning.

3. When using her weighted blanket and ear defenders, Isla will be able to sit and attend during assembly for 15 minutes.

FUTURE GOALS

1. Isla will use sensory supports to stay engaged in the classroom throughout the entire day.

2. Isla will arrive at school on time each day.

3. Isla will access music lessons.

Proposed plan
SCHEDULED STRATEGIES

1. Quiet reading in library on arrival to school each morning.

2. Heavy work circuit after break.

3. Yoga/meditation club at lunch.

4. Heavy work circuit before/after PE, music and art lessons.

ACCESSIBLE STRATEGIES

1. Heavy work corner in room.

2. Weighted blanket.

3. Surgical brush.

4. Ear defenders.

5. Quiet space – currently the sofa outside the business manager's office.

ADDITIONAL HOME SUPPORTS

- Isla's mum has found school uniforms she is comfortable wearing.

- Isla does 30 minutes of quiet reading when she first gets home from school.

- Isla cycles at least three times a week with her dad.

- Isla goes to a yoga and ballet class weekly during term time.

- Her parents ensure that there is sufficient down time at the weekend.

Monitoring

This is data that will be collected and compared over the term, before and after strategies have been used. It will be recorded using tally marks on a recording sheet which the school staff complete each day.

1. The number of times Isla goes to the toilet or hides under her desk when feeling overloaded or shut down stops her from joining in lessons. The number of times Isla accesses a sensory support to allow her to remain engaged.

2. The number of times Isla says she is not coming to school in

the morning to her mother. The number of times Isla is late to school.

3. The amount of time Isla spends in assembly each week.

Example sensory diet: Isla

8:15: Quiet reading in library

Assembly days, 9:00/9:30: Heavy work circuit

10:30: Heavy work circuit

12:00: Lunchtime yoga

PE/Music/Art days, 13:30: Heavy work circuit

15:30: Quiet reading at home on her beanbag

Always accessible: Ear defenders, quiet space, weighted blanket

Quiet space contains:

-   Sofa

-   Box containing a *Guinness Book of Records* and a piece of resistance band

-   Pictures of square breathing exercises

Heavy work circuit example:

-   Resistance band: Pull apart, pull from behind shoulders

-   Yoga poses: Warrior 2 and Chair

-   Wall press-ups x 10

-   Hand presses x 10

-   Repeat

Sensory passport: Isla

My name: Isla
My goals: 1. I will access sensory supports to lower my arousal 50% of the time when I become overloaded in the classroom. 2. I will come into school 90% of the time without complaint in the morning. 3. Using my weighted blanket and ear defenders, I will be able to sit and attend during assembly for 15 minutes.

My sensory preferences:	My sensory triggers:
Quiet spaces Touch pressure/proprioceptive input	Loud noises: whistle/bell/singing Low level noise over time: projector/class noise Being accidentally touched/bumped Some clothing/shoes Sticky textures: glue/tape/clay Making an error in my work Playground/PE

My communication supports: • See communication passport
My arousal

Arousal	I look like	This helps
0	I am engaged in my lessons I am smiling a lot I respond verbally to questions and ask questions in lessons I work mostly independently	Quiet reading in library each morning (S) Heavy work circuit after break (H) Yoga/meditation club at lunch (S) Heavy work circuit before/after assembly, PE, music and art lessons (S) Visual timetable and task plan (S) Adults checking in on my progress (S)

Red 3 Red 4/5	I become quieter I chew my collar or pencil I shut down (quiet, withdrawn, verbally unresponsive) I may hide under my desk or in the art cupboard	Heavy work activities (S) Weighted blanket (H) Touch pressure: hands on my shoulders (H) Surgical brush: on my arms (H) Ear defenders in noisy spaces (S) Quiet space (S) Reading my *Guinness Book of Records* (S) Visual plan now/next (S)
Yellow 3 Yellow 4/5	I jump up and down I flap my hands I jump and spin	Touch pressure: hands on my shoulders (H) Surgical brush: on my arms (H) Heavy work activities (S)
Blue 3 Blue 4/5	I start to cry I rock myself back and forth I shut down (quiet, withdrawn, verbally unresponsive)	Weighted blanket (H) Reading my *Guinness Book of Records* (S) My soft fluffy bear – 'Fluffy' (kept in cupboard next to door in classroom) (S) Visual plan now/next (S)
Green 3 Green 4/5	I yawn I become quieter I sleep (very rarely seen in school)	Quiet space (S) Taking a nap (S)
S = I can use this strategy by myself. **H** = I need help from an adult to use this strategy.		

Case Study 2: Noah

Noah is an eight-year-old boy with Down's syndrome. He really struggles to stay seated at his desk all day and often leans over or is slumped. He also finds it tricky to keep focused on what his teacher is saying when she talks for longer periods. He gets tired in the afternoon. Although he loves PE, he finds it hard to keep up with the other children and his balance is poor. He finds loud and unexpected sounds difficult to process and will run away if they occur. He can become overexcited if he has had too much movement, especially spinning.

Screening checklist: Noah
Part 1: Child's perspective

If the child is able to contribute, consider each of the senses with the child and what their preferences are.

	I find this easy/I enjoy	I find this tricky/I don't enjoy
Taste	I like chocolate	I don't like meat
Sounds/Noises		Police sirens Fire alarm
Sights	My glitter wand	
Touch	Big hugs	
Body awareness		Using my knife and fork
Balance/ Movement	I love running and being on the swing	Sitting still
Doing my work	Story time	Writing Maths

Part 2: Arousal contributors
EXTERNAL FACTORS

1. Environment sensations: Use the environmental checklist to help your analysis.

    • In which environments is the child successful? *The playground, lunchtime play.*

    • Which environments are more challenging? *Seated tasks.*

2. People: Consider relationships between adults and peers, and both positive and negative influencing factors.

    • Which relationships support the child? *Good relationship with all school staff.*

    • Which relationships are more challenging? *None.*

3. Tasks and activities.

    • With which tasks is the child successful? *Learning that*

includes physical experiences, lunch play with peers, forest school.

- Which tasks does the child find more challenging? *Noah's attainment is delayed across most subjects. He has additional support in place for this.*

4. Are there any other external stressors (e.g., new sibling, sick parents, unstable housing, exam period)? *Parents are separated, Noah spends every other Thursday to Sunday with his father. He is more dysregulated on the Monday following this because he is excited to see his mother and their pet dog that evening.*

INTERNAL FACTORS

1. Is the child aware of their internal body sensations? Can they manage these successfully? *Usually, but it took a long time for him to learn.*

2. What is the child's sleep like? *No issues when well, deteriorates significantly when he has a cold/blocked sinus.*

3. Are there any internal stressors (e.g., personal expectations, perfectionism)? *No.*

4. What motivates the child to succeed? *Noah loves forest school and helping in forest school and with the gardening at school.*

5. Is there a diagnosis that needs to be considered? *Down's syndrome.*

6. Do communication skills need to be considered? *Yes, see speech therapy report/summary. Noah uses Makaton to support his communication.*

HISTORY

1. Cumulative sensations: Consider what has occurred beforehand and the sensations across the day. *This is only an issue if there has been a loud unexpected sound, e.g., fire alarm.*

2. Previous experiences: Consider any previous experiences that might be impacting the child's participation and engagement. *None.*

3. Are there any adverse childhood experiences (e.g., trauma, neglect, poverty)? *Noah needed heart surgery when he was an infant, which resulted in long periods in and out of hospital before he was two years old and put a lot of stress on the family.*

Part 3: Sensory reactivity

Taste		
Sensitive	Slow	Seeking
• Gags when new foods are presented		

Smell		
Sensitive	Slow	Seeking
		• Smells people, animals and objects • Enjoys being close to people who wear perfume or cologne

Vision		
Sensitive	Slow	Seeking
		• Watches visually stimulating scenes (e.g., aquarium, spinning objects) • Chooses objects that are brightly coloured, including clothing • Likes to flip light switches on and off

Auditory (Sound/Noise)		
Sensitive	Slow	Seeking
• Dislikes loud, unexpected sounds (sirens, school bells) • Responds negatively to loud noises by running away, crying or holding hands over ears • Startles easily to unexpected sounds • Prefers to stay away from noisy settings • Fears music concerts or cinema or assembly/lunch hall (cafeteria)		

Tactile (Touch)		
Sensitive	Slow	Seeking
	• Has an unusually high tolerance for pain • Is unaware of temperature changes • May not notice if bumped or pushed	• Touches and feels objects • Touches people to the point of irritating them • Loves messy play

Proprioception (Body awareness)		
Sensitive	Slow	Seeking
	• Becomes tired easily, especially when standing or holding the body in one position • Leans on walls or slumps on furniture • Uses too much force, and can often break things as a result • Walks loudly as if feet are heavy • Is described as having 'weak muscles'	• Grinds teeth

Vestibular (Movement)		
Sensitive	Slow	Seeking
	• Bumps into things or falls over objects • Loses balance unexpectedly when walking on an uneven surface • Often has poor muscle tone (appears more floppy than others) • Has slow motor responses • Tires quickly/has poor endurance	• Likes jumping and crashing! • Likes moving, spinning and rolling! • Shows a strong preference for excessive spinning, swinging or rolling • Loves extreme fast-moving input (e.g., swings/slides/rollercoaster) • Rarely gets dizzy

Interoception

Consider the following.

Does the child recognize when they...? *Doesn't always recognize hot/cold. Doesn't identify when he is too excited.*

Do they:

- Ask for/get food when hungry? *Yes.*

- Ask for/get a drink when thirsty? *Yes.*

- Take off/put on their jumper if hot/cold? *With adult prompts.*

- Make it to the toilet with sufficient time (i.e., not at the last minute)? *Yes.*

- Rest when they are tired? *Yes.*

- Identify subtle changes in their emotions (e.g., when they are a little annoyed)? *Some challenges with excitement.*

- Speak to adults if they are stressed/worried? *Yes, to his ability.*

- Advise adults when they are feeling sick/unwell? *Yes.*

Part 4: Praxis/Posture

Dyspraxia		
Ideation	**Planning**	**Doing**
• Is repetitive with play • Watches others first before they start	• Has difficulty learning **new tasks**, including routines, steps, sports, daily activities • Has difficulty completing tasks with several steps • Has poor organization of materials and self • Completes activities in an awkward way	• Takes longer to do things • Has difficulty with activities containing more than one step • Is clumsy, accident prone • Trips up or bumps into people or things • Has difficulty with hopping, jumping, skipping or running compared to same-aged peers • Has poor skills in ball activities or other sports • Has difficulty with fine motor activities like buttons, writing and using scissors • Is untidy when eating

Postural control
• Has difficulty turning handles or taps that require some pressure • Has poor balance during motor activities and may fall over easily, sometimes even when seated • Has difficulty maintaining posture at the desk/table • Does not automatically move as necessary to complete physical tasks (e.g., does not shift over to catch a ball thrown to one side) • Has difficulty using both hands at the same time and may not consistently use their non-dominant hand to help • Tires easily or appears tired most of the time

Environmental checklist: Noah
Environment being assessed: Main classroom
Child's perspective – prompt for each sense if needed

Are there any sensations you find helpful in this room/space?
Noah really enjoys movement.

Are there any sensations you find distracting or tricky to manage in this room/space?
Loud/unexpected sounds.

Smell – *no concerns.*

Vision		
Check for	**Notes**	**Changes required**
Lighting • Flickering • Intensity if sitting under		
Reflections • Windows/shiny surfaces	Very distracted by them	Seat Noah away from the window
Distractions • Wall displays • Shadows/sunlight • Outdoor activity/ object • Preferred object • Clutter	Easily distracted, especially if there is an item of interest on the displays	Ensure that Noah's desk faces forward and wall displays are on the back walls He can use a privacy screen if he needs to when working

Sounds		
Check for	**Notes**	**Changes required**
Intrusive/unexpected sounds • Printer printing • School bell/whistles • Gardener	Noah is easily startled with loud/unexpected sounds	Warn Noah before all bells Lower pitch bird whistles to be used if needed in PE

Touch – *no specific issues.*

Proprioceptive		
Check for	**Notes**	**Changes required**
Space around the child • Proximity of others	Noah will lean on others when he becomes tired	Ensure there is sufficient space around him at carpet time Provide him with a Lycra body bag to give a boundary and additional feedback

Vestibular		
Check for	**Notes**	**Changes required**
Movement opportunities • Movement breaks	The usual classroom routine does not include many opportunities for movement	Add in additional movement breaks Create Move it Zone
Seating • Consider dynamic options • Consider sensitivity	Noah rocks on his chair and gets up to move about the classroom	Try Zuma rocker chair

Sensory planning: Noah
Reviewing the evaluation documents and information

Noah's vestibular and proprioceptive senses are slower to respond (hypo-reactive). This means his arousal decreases throughout the day. It also impacts his postural control and balance. He experiences sound sensitivity, and this must be considered when creating his sensory plan.

Noah is trying to engage in class but struggles when his arousal drops as he wants to move. He loves coming to school. Due to his diagnosis, Noah needs additional supports to access academic learning.

Goal setting

The primary goal for Noah is to help to increase his arousal level across the day to allow him to stay engaged at school. Because Noah can become quickly over-aroused if he has too much movement, proprioceptive sensory input will be included to help him to stay regulated.

CURRENT GOALS

1. With adult support, Noah will identify when he needs to increase his arousal during lessons. With adult support, Noah will access the 'Move it Zone' to help him to reorganize so he can complete his work.

FUTURE GOALS

1. Noah will independently identify when he needs to increase his arousal during lessons. Noah will independently access the 'Move it Zone' to help him to reorganize so he can complete his work.

2. Using the arousal bar, Noah will identify when his arousal is becoming too high during an activity and choose a strategy that will help him to calm down.

Proposed plan

SCHEDULED STRATEGIES

1. Zuma rocker

2. Movement breaks between lessons.

ACCESSIBLE STRATEGIES

1. 'Move it Zone' in classroom.

ADDITIONAL SUPPORTS

*   Noah attends occupational therapy which focuses on postural control and sensory responses using a sensory integration approach.

*   To help at home, his mother increased his physical activity to include football and scooting to school.

Monitoring

This is data that will be collected and compared over the term, before and after strategies have been used. It will be recorded using tally marks on a recording sheet which the school staff complete each day.

1. The number of times Noah gets up out of his desk to wander the classroom or interrupt others.

2. The amount of time Noah is spending focused on his work.

3. The number of times Noah uses the 'Move it Zone' to increase his arousal.

4. The number of times Noah becomes over-aroused during the day.

Example sensory diet: Noah

8:00: Cycling to school

9:00: Movement break with teaching assistant prior to phonics

10:00: Outdoor play circuit or playing football

11:00: Whole-class movement break prior to maths – using a dance video

12:00: Lunchtime play (this is never taken away as punishment)

13:30: Movement break with teaching assistant prior to learning (lessons vary)

15:15: Cycle home

Access to 'Move it Zone' through the day

Movement break example 1: Using the hall

- Run along long side, hop along short side, run along long side, jump along short side – repeat
- Yoga poses: Warrior 2 and Triangle
- Repeat run/hop/run/jump x 2
- Wall press-ups x 10

Movement break example 2: Using the corridor

- 20 seconds each of star jumps, running on the spot, jump side to side and twist
- Yoga poses: Chair and Frog
- Repeat twice

Sensory passport: Noah

My name: Noah

My goals:

1. With adult support, Noah will identify when he needs to increase his arousal during lessons.
2. With adult support, Noah will access the 'Move it Zone' to help him to reorganize so he can complete his work.

My sensory preferences:	My sensory triggers:
I love to move I like big hugs	Loud sounds Unexpected sounds Sitting still for long periods Sitting on the floor

My communication supports:

- Makaton when arousal is high

My arousal		
Arousal	**I look like**	**This helps**
0	Smiling Talking Listening to instructions Sitting in my chair	Zuma rocker (S) Movement breaks between lessons (H)
Red 3 **Red 4/5**	Body tenses Coordination decreases Less responsive to his name Crying/Wailing Refusing to move	Heavy work activities (S) Linear movement (e.g., head over ball) (H) Having a drink from my water bottle (S)
Yellow 3 **Yellow 4/5**	Giggling Bumping into others Starts spinning More giggling/spinning	Heavy work activities (S) Linear movement (e.g., head over ball) (H) Having a drink from my water bottle (S)
Blue 3 **Blue 4/5**	Goes quiet Withdraws Crying/Wailing Refusing to move	Linear movement (e.g., head over ball) (H) Having a drink from my water bottle (S) Being by myself with one other adult (no children in space) (S)

Green 3	Standing up, moving about Rocking in chair Not paying attention Interrupting others	Move it Zone sequences (S/H) • Jumping • Twisting/Down and up • Run on spot
Green 4/5	Slumping in desk	• Finish with press-up or yoga poses Movement Breaks/Zone – must **always finish** with press-ups or a yoga pose
S = I can use this strategy by myself. **H** = I need help from an adult to use this strategy.		

Helpful heavy work activities

- Press-ups (wall/floor/chair)

- Theraband

- Hand press/pull.

References

Ayres, J.A. (1973) *Sensory Integration and Learning Disorders*. Los Angeles, CA: Western Psychological Services.

Bialer, S. & Miller, L.J. (2011) *No Longer a Secret*. Arlington, TX: Future Horizons.

Biel, L. (2014) *Sensory Processing Challenges: Effective Clinical Work with Kids and Teens*. New York, NY: W.W. Norton & Company.

Bogdashina, O. (2003) *Sensory Perceptual Issues in Autism and Asperger Syndrome*. London: Jessica Kingsley Publishers.

Brackett, M.A., (2019) *Permission to Feel: Unlock the Power of Emotions to Help Yourself and Your Child Thrive* London: Quercus.

Bundy, A. & Lane, S. (2019) *Sensory Integration Theory and Practice*, 3rd Edition. Philadelphia, PA: FA Davis.

Chatterjee, R. (2018) *The Stress Solution*. London: Penguin Life.

Diagnostic and Statistical Manual of Mental Disorders: www.psychiatry.org/psychiatrists/practice/dsm

Dunn, W. (1999) *Sensory Profile 1st Edition*. London: Pearson.

Dunn, W. (2008) *Living Sensationally*. London: Jessica Kingsley Publishers.

Dunn, W. (2015) *Sensory Profile*, 2nd Edition. San Antonio, TX: Pearson Assessments.

Goodall, E. (2021) Facilitating interoceptive awareness as a self-management and self-regulation tool to increase engagement in learning and education (Doctoral dissertation, University of Southern Queensland). https://eprints.usq.edu.au/42829

Goodall, E. & Brownlow, C. (2022) *Interoception and Regulation: Teaching Skills of Body Awareness and Supporting Connection with Others*. London: Jessica Kingsley Publishers.

Grace, J. (2019) *Multiple Multi-Sensory Rooms: Myth Busting the Magic*. London: Routledge.

Griffin, K. & Allen, S. (2021) *Auditing the impact of online sensory processing training for educators, families, and professionals*. www.griffinot.com/the-impact-of-sensory-processing-with-griffin-ot

International Classification of Diseases: https://icd.who.int

Kirby, A. & Sugden, D.A. (2007) Children with developmental coordination disorders. *Journal of the Royal Society of Medicine*, 100(4), 182–186. https://doi.org/10.1177/014107680710011414

Kranowitz, C. (2005) *The Out-of-Sync Child*. New York, NY: Penguin Putnam.

Lombard, A. (2015) *Sensory Intelligence: Why it Matters More than IQ and EQ*. Welgemoed, South Africa: Metz Press.

Maslow, A.H. (1943) A theory of human motivation. *Psychological Review*, 50(4), 370–396.

Miller, L.J. (2014) *Sensational Kids: Hope and Help for Children with Sensory Processing Disorder (SPD) – Revised*. New York, NY: TarcherPerigee.

Mucklow, N. (2010) *The Sensory Team Handbook*. Book Baby.

National Institute for Health and Care Excellence (2017) Autism spectrum disorder in under 19s: recognition, referral and diagnosis: www.nice.org.uk/guidance/cg128

Ockwell-Smith, S. (2015) *The Gentle Sleep Book*. London: Hachette.

Parham, D., Ecker, C., Miller Kuhaneck, H., Henry, H.M. & Glennon, T. (2007) *Sensory Processing Measure*. Los Angeles, CA: Western Psychological Services.

Perry, B.D. & Winfrey, O. (2021) *What Happened to You? Conversations on Trauma, Resilience and Healing*. New York, NY: Flatiron Books.

Posner, J., Russell, J., & Peterson, B. (2005). The circumplex model of affect: An integrative approach to affective neuroscience, cognitive development, and psychopathology. *Development and Psychopathology, 17*(3), 715-734. doi:10.1017/S0954579405050340

Royal College of Occupational Therapists (2019) *Unlocking the Potential of Children and Young People*. www.rcot.co.uk/ilsm

Russell, James. (1980). A Circumplex Model of Affect. Journal of Personality and Social Psychology. 39, 1161-1178. https://doi.org/10.1037/h0077714

Russell, J.A. (2008) The Circumplex Model of Affect: An Integrative Approach to Affective Neuroscience, Cognitive Development, and Psychopathology. In J. Posner, J.A. Russell & B.S. Peterson, *Development and Psychopathology*. https://doi.org/10.1017/S0954579405050340

Sapolsky, R. (2004) *Why Zebras Don't Get Ulcers*. New York, NY: Holt Paperbacks.

Siegel, D. & Payne Bryson, T. (2012) *The Whole-Brain Child*. London: Robinson.

Shanker, Dr. S. (2016) *Self-Reg: How to Help Your Child (and You) Break the Stress Cycle and Successfully Engage with Life*. London: Penguin Books.

Shanker, Dr. S. & Hopkins, S. (2019) *Self-Reg Schools: A Handbook for Educators*. London: Penguin Books.

van der Kolk, B. (2014) *The Body Keeps the Score: Brain, Mind and Body in the Healing of Trauma*. London and New York, NY: Penguin Publishing Group.

Voss, A. (2015) *Understanding Your Child's Sensory Signals*. Create Space Independent Publishing Platform.

Walker, M. (2017) *Why We Sleep*. New York, NY: Scribner.

Webb, C. (2016) *How to Have a Good Day*. London: Macmillan.

Glossary

Arousal: The level of energy and alertness in the body. At its simplest, it is how alert or asleep your body is in any given moment.

Co-regulation: When someone else helps the child to regulate.

Discriminative touch: This part of our touch system provides very specific and detailed information about what we are touching or where we have been touched. It helps us to understand the shape and texture of items. It facilitates our fine motor skills and dexterity.

Dyspraxia: Difficulty planning, organizing and sequencing new movements or activities.

Emotional regulation: The ability to regulate our emotional responses.

Fight, flight, freeze: A response that the body's nervous system has when it is in danger, or it perceives it is in danger.

Interoception: The final internal sense, which processes internal sensory messages received from our organs, hormones and immune system. These messages tell the brain about what's going on inside the body and help it to understand the body's internal state.

Over-arousal: Occurs when a child's arousal is too high.

Proprioception: Often called our 'hidden sixth sense'. Our proprioceptors, which are located in our muscles and joints, let the brain know where our limbs are in space and how they are moving. Essentially, proprioception helps you to 'feel' where your body is.

Protective touch: A light touch sensation; for example, a spider's web touching your skin, or hair touching your face. As the name suggests, protective touch plays a key role in keeping us safe, and protecting us.

This type of touch is very alerting and can produce a fight, flight, freeze response.

Regulation: The ability to adjust and change your level of arousal to match the demands of a task and the environment. For example, if you are running late, your arousal will increase due to stress. Once you reach your destination the brain should lower your arousal and help you to recover. The brain is constantly regulating our state of arousal throughout the day, often unconsciously.

Self-regulation: The ability to stay regulated without the help of others. It is the ability to use strategies independently to either calm down or energize.

Sensory discrimination: Processing of the qualities of the sensory message. It refers to what, how and where. What was the sensation? How intense was it? Where did it occur?

Sensory integration theory: The original theory proposed by Dr A. Jean Ayres and built on by other therapists. It explores how the brain processes sensory information to produce a response.

Sensory integration treatment: A specific treatment approach designed by Dr Ayres. To separate it from other approaches, it is now called Ayres® Sensory Integration. This approach should only be provided by trained therapists who have completed additional post-graduate training.

Sensory overload: Occurs when a child has received too much sensory information. It is commonly reported by those who experience over-responsivity (hyper-reactivity) and by autistic individuals.

Sensory passport: A short one- to two-page document that outlines a student's goals, preferences, triggers, arousal state indicators and support strategies. It is a quick reference tool that staff can use.

Sensory reactivity: The intensity with which an individual's brain interprets the sensory messages it receives. Everyone has different thresholds to sensory information, and this influences how their brain reacts. Reactivity affects our responses and our capacity to respond to and engage with learning. Some authors call sensory reactivity **sensory modulation**.

Sensory registration: The moment the brain registers or recognizes that a sensation has occurred. Registration is the 'a ha!' moment, the moment the brain notices the sensation.

Sensory sensitivity (over-responsivity/hyper-reactivity): When the brain interprets sensory messages with a greater level of intensity.

Sensory slow (under-responsivity/hypo-reactivity): When the brain is slower to interpret sensory messages as it perceives them with less intensity. These children often need more sensory inputs to process the information. Sometimes they will seek out additional sensory inputs themselves.

Sensory stimming: Repetitive movements or actions which autistic children make. Common stims include hand flapping, looking persistently out of the corners of the eye, watching spinning objects, and jumping. Some children may also have vocal stims where they repeat phrases or sounds.

Sensory strategies: Supports or equipment that use the senses to help organize arousal levels and engagement in activity. Examples include wobble cushions, fidget toys, touch pressure or heavy work, a sensory diet or a sensory circuit. They are commercially readily available. No specific training is required to use sensory strategies. However, the more informed you are, the more success you will have in using them.

Shut down: A freeze response in relation to sensory overload. The brain shuts down in order to protect itself and to be able to manage in the situation. The child may be unresponsive. When this occurs, the child will need time and access to a space or strategy that they find helps them to calm down.

Specialist supports: Strategies delivered by therapists (like an occupational therapist or speech and language therapist) or highly trained staff (like the special educational needs and disabilities coordinator or therapy assistant). These supports are very specific to an individual child. Most readers of this book will not be delivering specialist supports.

Targeted supports: Strategies or supports designed for individuals or groups. They are not necessarily available to all children. Staff implementing them have usually received some training; this might be from a specialist teacher or from a therapist. Or they might read a book like this! In some special schools, targeted supports may be more universally available.

Universal supports: Strategies or supports that are in place for every child in the school. They are the foundation supports which help to create a consistent and clear space for children. Universal supports are something that every team member in a school should be able to implement. They are the non-negotiables which are always in place.

Vestibular sense: Usually called the balance sense. The receptors for the vestibular sense are in the middle ear, after the cochlea, in a section called the vestibule. The receptors are activated by head movement. They tell the brain how fast the head is moving, in which direction and how high it is off the ground.

Index